RASANAH
المعهد الدولي للدراسات الإيرانية
International Institute for Iranian Studies

IRAN'S POLICIES TOWARD CENTRAL ASIA AND THE CAUCASUS

*Investing in Opportunities
and Ousting Competitors*

Dr. Ahmed Daifullah al-Garni

Translated by
Ruba Taha Abu-Mualish

PARTRIDGE

King Fahd National Library Cataloging-in-Publication Data

ISBN:	Hardcover	978-1-5437-8210-3
	Softcover	978-1-5437-8208-0
	eBook	978-1-5437-8209-7

Translated from Arabic by Abu Mualish, Ruba Taha

Print information available on the last page.

To order additional copies of this book, contact
Toll Free +65 3165 7531 (Singapore)
Toll Free +60 3 3099 4412 (Malaysia)
orders.singapore@partridgepublishing.com

www.partridgepublishing.com/singapore

CONTENTS

INTRODUCTION 1

CHAPTER ONE: CENTRAL ASIA AND THE
CAUCASUS — IRAN'S STRATEGIC PERSPECTIVE.........5

Geographical and Historical Imperatives in Central Asia
and the Caucasus — the Iranian Perspective.............................6

Objectives and Premises of Iran's Foreign Policy Toward
Central Asia and the South Caucasus.......................................15

Security Dimensions of Iran's Relations With Central
Asia and the South Caucasus...18

CHAPTER TWO: IRAN'S SOFT POWER TOOLS:
CULTURE AND IDEOLOGY...25

Iran's Policy Toward the Region's Secular Governments.............26

Limits of Iran's Soft Power 28

Exploitation of Cultural Heritage and Nationalistic
Calculations 36

CHAPTER THREE: IRAN'S ECONOMIC AND
TRADE TIES WITH CENTRAL ASIA AND
THE SOUTH CAUCASUS 45

Dispute Over Caspian Sea Resources 46

Iran's Project to Exploit Oil Resources in the Caspian Sea 52

Trade Between Iran and Central Asia 57

International North–South Transport Corridor............................63

CHAPTER FOUR: COUNTRIES COMPETING
WITH IRAN FOR INFLUENCE IN CENTRAL
ASIA AND THE CAUCASUS 71

Russia...72

The United States...76

China 79

Turkey 81

Israel..84

The Kingdom of Saudi Arabia 85

CONCLUSION 89

ENDNOTES 93

ABOUT THE AUTHOR 103

INTRODUCTION

Whoever gains control of Central Asia gains control over the Eurasia continent; whoever controls Eurasia gains control over the world

Halford Mackinder

The landmass of Central Asia and the Caucasus was referred to as the "World Island" by British geographer Halford Mackinder. He asserted, "Whoever gains control of Central Asia gains control over the Eurasia continent; whoever controls Eurasia gains control over the world." In geographical terms, this landmass is known as Central Eurasia.

Central Asia and the South Caucasus are of vital importance; global and regional powers pay significant attention to both regions — given their strategically important locations. Both possess pivotal oil and gas pipeline corridors and extensive natural resources. Their political, economic and geographical characteristics make them significant in the context of international relations.

Following the collapse of the Soviet Union, the Central Asian countries achieved independence and emerged as an arena for global and regional competition for influence. A host of countries have been vying to play a broader role in Central Asia; namely Russia which has reemerged as a great power; China which is seeking to dominate the global economy and trade relations; the United States which is attempting to limit the expansion of Russia and Iran; the EU which is looking for economic partners and oil supplies; and finally Israel and Turkey given their national, economic and security considerations.

Given its geographical location bordering Central Asia and its shared historical bonds and challenges, Iran is competing for influence in the region with the intention to invest in emerging opportunities. However, Iran has shunned the idea of triggering any military confrontation in the region and has only deployed its soft power tools. The country is fully aware of the limits of its hard power compared to that of Russia and the United States. The independence of the Central Asian countries has presented opportunities as well as challenges to Iran. The latter include addressing the mounting influence of global powers in the Central Asian countries and the potential threats arising from instability in them. Bordering the region makes it obligatory for Iran to protect its borders, as some of these countries have been suffering from border instability since the collapse of the Soviet Union. Iran is fully aware of the need to avoid any border dispute in the future or any clash with Russia as it has been attempting to fill the gap in Central Asia following the collapse of the Soviet Union.

Based on the aforementioned, the book discusses Iran's role and presence in Central Asia and the South Caucasus as well as bringing to the fore the opportunities and challenges facing Tehran in these regions. The book aims to answer a series of important questions:

• What is the significance of these regions in the context of Iran's strategic perspective?

• What is the extent of Iran's ideological and political influence in these regions?

• Do Iranian attempts to export the principles of the Khomeinist revolution pose a serious threat to the secular nature of the countries in these regions — as repeatedly echoed by the region's political leaders?

• To what extent will Iran benefit in terms of oil and non-oil commerce from these regions?

• Will Iran's strengthening of ties with these regions contribute to facilitating its expansionist tendencies in the Middle East?

The book investigates in detail the aforementioned questions to reveal Iran's strategic perspectives and the historical bedrock which it depends on to deal with the Central Asian countries. It also examines Iran's methods to expand its political influence such as using its ideological and cultural bonds to control the vital sphere of Central Asia. Finally, the book reviews Iran's economic and trade ties with Central Asia, analyzing its competition with global powers whose ambitions clash with those of Tehran. Global and regional powers aim to solely take control of Central Asia's natural resources or expand their influence in one of the most significant regions in the modern world. Iran realizes well the potential political, economic and strategic benefits once it achieves these two aforementioned objectives — or at least one of them.

Chapter One

CENTRAL ASIA AND THE CAUCASUS — IRAN'S STRATEGIC PERSPECTIVE

Geographical and Historical Imperatives in Central Asia and the Caucasus — the Iranian Perspective

Central Asia and the Caucasus are deemed important because of their geopolitical and geo-cultural considerations, with both regions viewed as the golden key to controlling the world. Securing a foothold in Central Asia enables easy access with minimal costs for all neighboring countries: whether Russia's strategic depth toward the north; China's strategic depth in the southeast, Iran's strategic depth toward the southwest, the Indian subcontinent toward the south, and the entire strategic depth of the Caspian Sea region toward the west. Establishing dominion over Central Asia's resources helps to achieve control over the supply of oil, gas, minerals and agricultural products to Russia, China, the Indian subcontinent and the EU. On the other hand, taking control of Central Asia's routes helps in securing influence over key land and water routes and other significant routes and roads that contribute to controlling the level of interactions and interrelations between Central Asia's neighboring countries.[1]

Needless to mention, in addition to its highly significant geographical location, Central Asia possesses natural resources of relatively high value such as oil, gas, uranium, minerals and water, reflecting its strategic value. Such natural wealth has made the region a battlefield for influence between great powers over several historical phases; for example "The Great Game;" a confrontation which continued throughout the 19th century between the British Empire and the Russian Empire. The region has reassumed its former status as a competitive arena in the struggle for influence between contemporary great powers along with regional powers in the current period. [2]

The Caucasus, a vast mountainous area located between the Black Sea and the oil rich Caspian Sea, enjoys a unique geographical location, bordering Russia, Iran and Turkey. The Caucasus is divided into two distinct geographical areas: the North Caucasus and the South Caucasus. The North Caucasus is entirely located within the former Soviet Union territories and includes self-governing republics: Adygea, Karachay-Cherkessia, Kabardino-Balkaria, North Ossetia, Chechnya, Ingushetia and Dagestan. The South Caucasus includes three independent republics: Georgia, Azerbaijan and Armenia (see Map 1.1).[3] These republics were completely under Soviet rule in the 1960s and achieved independence in 1991. In the same year, they joined the Commonwealth of Independent States (CIS).

Map 1.1: Central Asia and the Caucasus

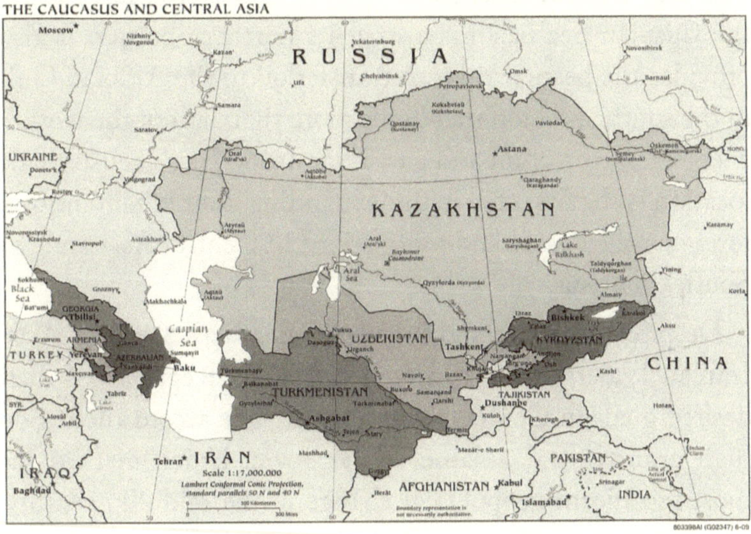

Source: Loyola University Chicago.[4]

The book discusses the South Caucasus, in particular Armenia and Azerbaijan, which not only share geographical proximity with Iran but also significant economic and cultural bonds. The North Caucasus is not included in the book because it is a Russian self-governed region. Central Asia, in the book, refers to the political region spanning five republics: Kazakhstan, Turkmenistan, Uzbekistan, Tajikistan and Kyrgyzstan. Central Asia stretches from the eastern part of the Caspian Sea to Mongolia's borders between China and Russia. It also extends from northern Afghanistan to the southern borders of Russia. Historically speaking, the region was previously called Turkistan but was renamed Central Asia after it joined the former Soviet Union during Joseph Stalin's rule. The region consists of five republics and covers an area of nearly 4 million square kilometers; 29.5 percent of the entire area of the Arab world.[5]

Iran sits at the crossroads of Asia between the Middle East and Central Asia, enjoying geopolitical significance and the Caspian Sea basin is also at its northern border. It also provides the best corridor to transfer oil to the Arabian Gulf in the south; a region that holds more than half of the world's energy reserves of oil and gas. Examining Iran's geostrategic location is the first step in understanding Tehran's intentions, foreign policy goals and motivations in Central Asia and the South Caucasus.

Despite the longstanding warm ties with Central Asia, Iranian leaders never had well-defined perceptions of their desired goals in Central Asia, nor did they accord the region high priority. The collapse of the Soviet Union marked the most significant geopolitical change in the mid 20th century, opening the gate for new Iranian perspectives in relation to its security and national interests. It is worthy of note that the majority of the Caspian Sea population is Sunni, but the region is also influenced by the sects and religions present across Iran's spheres of influence. Thus, it is difficult to specifically outline the cultural differences between the Iranian people and other peoples in Central Asia as they have longstanding historical bonds dating back to thousands of years, although these have gradually weakened since the Tsarist era.[6]

The Iranians believe that Russia's hegemony in the Caucasus in particular was established relatively late; the Russians dominated for nearly 200 years during the 18th century while the Persians spread their influence over a number of centuries in this region. The Persian presence under the ancient and Islamic empires penetrated deep into the identity fabric of this region, creating a Persian melting pot. Following the collapse of the Soviet Union, Iranian institutions worked to highlight this longstanding shared cultural identity while promoting the so-called "Great Iran" which is heavily based on the shared culture, history and economy with the peoples of the Caucasus. The Iranians aimed to find a pretext for their expansionist inclinations by reviving the ideas of shared identity and nationalism, especially with the Caucasus. It is worth recalling that Persian culture and nationalism during Islamic rule had a profound cultural and economic influence on the Caucasus.[7]

In modern times, specifically in the aftermath of World War II, Iran's relationship with the region can be divided into four periods as follows:[8]

First period (1945-1972): This period witnessed a conflict between the Iranian shah and the Soviet Union. It first started with the Iran crisis of 1946, also known as the Azerbaijan Crisis; which erupted after the refusal of Stalin's Red Army to withdraw from the occupied territories in northern Iran (1945-1946). During this period, Iran was addressing growing Soviet expansionism; it joined the Baghdad Pact and received arms from the United States.

Second period (1972-1978): The shah successfully adopted a positive balance policy; playing a mediating role between the East and West. Through this policy, which made Iran the region's policeman, it entered a new phase in the Cold War. However, it established trade and cultural relations with many countries in the Eastern bloc.

Third period (1978-1991): This period is marked by the rise of the "Islamic Republic of Iran" and its foreign policy motto "Neither East, nor West, Islamic Republic." The Soviet Union, back then, took steps to strengthen relations with the new Iranian revolutionary government that helped in expelling the biggest US military and political base stationed in the Soviet neighborhood.

The Soviets were fully aware of the potential backlash from the 50 million Muslims living inside their territories bordering Iran and were concerned that the new Iranian revolutionary and theocratic-determined ideology would attract them. The Soviets exerted all efforts possible to keep Muslims away from any official contact with the new Iran. The 1979 revolution was a critical turning point in Iran's contemporary political history and impacted the country's foreign policy in the region.

Fourth period (the post-Soviet era): By late 1991, the world witnessed the collapse of the Soviet Union and several republics declared their independence. Such dramatic shifts cast a long shadow on Iran's foreign policy toward the newly independent Islamic republics, given the fact that Iran had played an integral role in the region. Iran exerted all efforts to fill the power vacuum resulting from the Soviet Union's collapse; its top priority — back then — was to expand its economic, cultural and political ties with the region's countries. Later, it intensified its role, which directly coincided with Turkey's growing interest in the region; Ankara declared its Baku-Tbilisi-Ceyhan export pipeline project, which is directly related to Ankara's ambition to establish a "Greater Turkey" in the region.

During the Iran-Iraq War, the pace of Iran's foreign policy in the region slowed as the Iranian government was occupied with economic and social fallouts at home. The northern front was not a top priority back then. After the war ended, Iran was keen to quickly bounce back from the ashes of the war. The Iranian government replaced its old foreign policy mantra of "Neither East, Nor West" with "Both North and South," as announced by the former late Iranian President Hashemi Rafsanjani. This new policy called on the Iranian government to boost its relations with the newly independent republics in Central Asia and the Caucasus. Rafsanjani affirmed in 1992 that Iran was a role model for the region's countries, adding that his country viewed its relations with the new republics not from the prism of "The Great Game."[9]

Iran emerged as a key player in the Caspian Sea basin after the collapse of the Soviet Union and the establishment of the three littoral republics of the Caspian Sea — Azerbaijan, Kazakhstan and Turkmenistan, which called for sovereignty over their territorial waters. During the Soviet era, the oil fields in the Caspian Sea were not exploited. Iran's activities back then were merely focused on fishing and the lucrative export of caviar. When oil was discovered; the strategic significance of the region mounted, fueling Iran's ambitions to play a major role — given the fact that it had already established relatively advanced oil facilities there. Iran aimed to be the major transporter of Caspian Sea oil through its territory to the Arabian Gulf.[10]

The late R.K. Ramazani who was a distinguished professor at the Woodrow Wilson Department of Politics, the University of Virginia, explained that in the post-Khomeini era, Iran's foreign policy motto "Neither East, nor West," gradually diminished and was replaced by Rafsanjani's "Both North and South."[11] Iran, since then, has depended on the latter to develop its foreign policy, whether for economic or political reasons, with its Caspian Sea neighbors. Iran's foreign policy architects have always deemed their country's unique location as a bridge between the Arabian Gulf and the Caspian Sea. They believe that this location enables Iran to play a consistent role in the political, social and economic developments in the region. Iran's interactions with the region's countries started even before the recognition of their independence from the Soviet Union in December 1991. Iran had concluded in November 1991 agreements with Turkmenistan and Azerbaijan to open new border crossings. During the same month, Iran's former Foreign Minister Ali Akbar Velayati paid a 10-day visit to the region and concluded agreements to inaugurate Iranian consulates in all of the region's countries as well as to open embassies in Azerbaijan, Tajikistan, Turkmenistan, Kazakhstan and Armenia in early 1992; Uzbekistan and Kyrgyzstan in May; and Georgia in June of the same year.[12]

Given the new geopolitical realities, Russia no longer borders Iran's northern border. Now, Iran shares a 1,740-kilometer border with Armenia, Turkmenistan and Azerbaijan and a 630-kilometer border adjacent to the Caspian Sea. The long border, rough terrain and history of long standing disputes with Russia, which still exist in the Caspian Sea, prompted Iran to avoid inciting any conflict in Central Asia and instead Tehran aimed to establish economic integration and partnerships to help boost stability and security. Iran has realized the value of the aforementioned geopolitical developments and has been eager to exploit them through establishing political, economic, trade and cultural ties with the region's countries, leveraging its location and history to play a broader role in the region. Through this rapprochement, Iran aims to break its Western imposed political isolation and to reposition itself in the region to have great influence not only in Central Asia but also in the Middle East.

With ambitions to deepen its political relations in the region, Iran has continuously submitted oil project proposals since 2001. Former Iranian Foreign Minister Kamal Kharazi stressed that "the region is a priority for Iran's foreign policy."[13] Ali Shamkhani, the former Iranian defense minister, logistical support officer and former secretary general of Iran's Supreme National Security Council said, "The collapse of the Soviet Union created opportunities for Iran's national security and interests but this shift has also opened the gate for other actors to enter the region; including Israel and the United States."[14]

It was to Iran's benefit that the new Central Asian republics strived to free themselves of Russia's influence through diversifying their economies and securing access to the open seas in the south. They viewed Iran as a key partner to achieve this goal despite increasing US pressure not to establish strong ties with Tehran. They, however, attempted to benefit from the economic and trade opportunities offered by Iran but at the same time, halt any potential export of Iran's "Islamic Revolution" that would risk their secular systems.

To expand its sectarian networks of influence across the region, Iran adopted a host of policies and approaches such as repairing shrines and mosques, launching cultural trips to Khomeini's shrine in southern Tehran and Imam Reza's shrine in Mashhad. However, Iran failed to gain traction in the region, most likely because of the cautious outlook of the region's governments when dealing with the Iranian government. This caution stemmed from the fact that the region's leaders embraced secular orientations and were concerned about the penetration of religious extremism into their countries. Further, their constitutions stipulate the separation of religion from the state, as a result they imposed strict restrictions on Iran and closely monitored religious activities in their countries.[15] Iran therefore resorted to craft a gradual, pragmatic policy that did not explicitly focus on exporting its revolutionary model but rather focused on promoting a pragmatic Persian model of governance. Iran did not work to spread its revolutionary ideology across Central Asia because of the sectarian differences and its realization that the region's ruling elites were secular and would reject its revolutionary ideology.[16]

Iran also took into consideration the ethnic tensions in the region and sought to gear such tensions and divisions to serve its interests by continuously emphasizing the shared cultural and ethnic identity. In his 1997 book *The Grand Chessboard: American Primacy and Its Geostrategic Imperatives*, Zbigniew Brzezinski, the former US national security advisor to the Carter administration, described Central Asia as the "Eurasian Balkans,"[17] comparing it to the former Yugoslavia which experienced hostile conflicts. Ethnic strife and divisions not only risk national unity and cohesion of the region's countries but also destabilize their intertwined relations. In the context of the aforementioned, Iran was aware of all realities and variables that would help in its quest to expand its dominance and influence in the region.

Iran's decision-makers adopted an approach of appeasement to ensure and convince the Central Asian republics that friendship with Iran was better than confrontation. To dispel their fears regarding its creeping revolutionary ideology, Iran adopted a pragmatic policy toward the region that varied from one republic to another. This policy focused on development, commercial partnerships and maintained as much as possible Iran's cultural and religious influence under the guise of cultural exchanges; specifically through cultural offices run by the IRGC and intelligence apparatuses.

Objectives and Premises of Iran's Foreign Policy Toward Central Asia and the South Caucasus

Iran's foreign policy toward Central Asia and the Caucasus is based on a host of considerations. Central Asia is of critical importance to Iran as several of its interests conflict or converge with the interactions of influential regional and international powers. The region has a wealth of diverse natural resources and is culturally in harmony with Iran's history and identity. Representing a form of strategic depth for Iran, the region offers golden opportunities and options for Iran to tackle its rising challenges.[18] Iran therefore seeks to align itself more closely with the Central Asian republics. It is keen to enhance security and stability in the region and avoid the eruption of ethnic strife, which will risk its own security and economy. Iran's leadership has laid down a host of strategic objectives to pursue in the region, most notably as follows:[19]

• Strengthening Iran's economic interests in Central Asia and the Caucasus through establishing oil projects as well as gas and oil pipelines given its extensive experience in the oil industry; investing in the region as it offers new markets for Iranian exports and a corridor to access the Black Sea and Europe; exploiting its strategic location as a transport link between the Caucasus and the Arabian Gulf (transporting the Caucasus' exports to the Arabian Gulf, then to the world).

• Enhancing security and stability in the region and avoiding the eruption of ethnic strife that will risk Iran's security and stability; defusing cross-border ethnic tensions that constitute a serious concern for Iran as various minority groups culturally extend into its territories such as the Kurds, Azeris, Turkmens and Armenians.

• Breaking Iran's international political isolation through establishing new allies in the region; actualized by taking Russia and Armenia as allies to oppose US policy, which uses Turkey and Azerbaijan to expand its influence in the region.

• Depriving competitors of any potential opportunity for success in the region, namely Turkey because of its pan-Turanism ambitions that proclaim the need to unite all Turkic peoples, and Saudi Arabia because of its potential Sunni influence in the region as it is considered the focal point of Sunni Islam.

• Forming pro-Iran geopolitical approaches that counter and diminish the interventions of Iran's rivals in its neighboring regions, especially the United States which aims to expand NATO's presence to the Caspian Sea basin.

It can be argued that Iran has intensified its initiatives to entrench its political superiority in the region, yet it is also extremely keen to maintain its economic interests. One week after the establishment of the CIS in 1991, Tehran rushed to open embassies in the newly independent Central Asian republics, commenced importing Azeri products and coordinated efforts with Azerbaijan, Kazakhstan and Turkmenistan on oil exploration in the Caspian Sea. The five independent republics represent huge potential markets, which Iran can also export its technology to.[20]

At the time, Mohsen Aminzadeh, Iran's then deputy foreign minister for Asia-Pacific and the CIS, outlined Iran's geo-economic shift, "Iran, today, is not a country that prefers the West over the Soviet Union. The dangers of the great rivalry over the north to access warm waters have vanished. It turned out positive; now we have five neighbors that cannot access warm waters but through our route."[21]

Iran's geo-economic location changed when the Soviet Union collapsed; it became a linking corridor between the Caspian Sea basin and the Arabian Gulf, needless to mention that its unique location has acquired greater significance in light of the geopolitics of energy.

In 2003 and 2008, Iran strongly supported the formation of an Asian alliance and called on Russia, India and the Central Asian republics to join it. It did not aim to merely mobilize the major world energy producers but to also galvanize human capital and forge a counterweight to the United States. Speaking at the Persian summit to the leaders of Afghanistan and Tajikistan, then Iranian President Mahmoud Ahmadinejad proposed the creation of a regional organization of exclusively Persian-speaking countries in April 2010.[22]

For three decades, Iran has sought to join regional organizations that include countries from Central Asia and the Caucasus, aiming to deepen its cooperation with these countries and use such organizations to conclude agreements in the fields of trade, energy, culture and security. The main regional organizations include the following:

• The Economic Cooperation Organization (ECO) is an intergovernmental regional organization established in 1985 by Iran, Pakistan and Turkey to strengthen economic, technological and cultural cooperation between member countries. In 1992, Afghanistan and six former Soviet republics: Azerbaijan, Kazakhstan, Kyrgyzstan, Tajikistan, Turkmenistan and Uzbekistan also joined the ECO. [23]

• The Shanghai Cooperation Organization (SCO) is an intergovernmental organization founded in 2001 by six countries: China, Russia, Kazakhstan, Kyrgyzstan, Tajikistan and Uzbekistan with an aim to promote cooperation in the fields of economy, security and culture[24] and to counterbalance the influence of the United States and NATO in the region.

In 2017, Pakistan and India joined the organization.[25] Iran gained observer status in 2005; since then, it has exerted all efforts possible to become a full member, but it failed despite repeated promises from some member countries, especially Russia, to grant it full membership after the lifting of sanctions. Sanctions were lifted in 2016 but the SCO did not grant Iran full membership. During the latest SCO summits, Russia and China supported Iran's full membership. Despite its previous support for Iran's full membership, Tajikistan began to oppose its inclusion as Dushanbe accused it of supporting the Islamic Renaissance Party of Tajikistan, also known as the Islamic Revival Party of Tajikistan, which is listed as a terrorist outfit by the Tajik government.

Security Dimensions of Iran's Relations With Central Asia and the South Caucasus

In the context of security considerations, Iran attempted to establish bonds of trust with the countries of Central Asia and the South Caucasus to evade any potential threats from their side; and control their ethnic, ideological and nationalist movements to save itself from their ramifications whether ethnic, security or economic in case of potential instability, resulting in waves of migration.

Iran has adopted a multidimensional approach to establish valuable relations with the Central Asian and Caucasus countries. Former Iranian Foreign Minister Ali Akbar Velayati pointed out that "Iran could not have remained passive in the face of deteriorating security conditions on its northern border after the collapse of the Soviet Union system."[26] As a result, Iran closed its borders and sought, at the same time, to enhance regional security and independence from its neighbors along the Caspian Sea.

Iran deems regional security and stability as an integral part of its national security.[27] Hence, it proposed the launch of several cooperation initiatives from 1992 to 1994. Some of these proved fruitful such as the memorandum of understanding concluded between the late Iranian President Hashemi Rafsanjani and his counterparts in Azerbaijan, Kazakhstan, Russia and Turkmenistan in February 1992 to establish a cooperation organization of the Caspian Sea countries. The organization aimed to "better handle the geopolitical situation of the region."[28] He laid the bedrock for future cooperation in the fields of fishing, environmental protection, maritime routes, pollution control and oil exploitation. However, the formal structure of Rafsanjani's proposed organization was never established, nevertheless, it clearly revealed Iran's new constructive approach toward its Caspian neighbors. The lack of a formal structure did not prevent Iran from developing diplomatic relations. On August 12, 2006, a legally binding treaty concluded by the five Caspian states came into force to protect the Caspian Sea environment.[29]

As for Iran, border conflicts are sources of security concern against the backdrop of geographical realities; Iran shares long borders with Turkmenistan, Armenia and Azerbaijan. A border conflict would destabilize Iran because it would find itself obliged to side with one party in the conflict. Iran was a major party in the Nagorno-Karabakh conflict; a territorial dispute between Armenia and Azerbaijan (see Map 1.2). It backed Armenia, risking its relations with Azerbaijan.[30] Some have argued that Iran is a strategic ally of Armenia against Azerbaijan; however, Iran explicitly sought to play a "diplomatic balancing act" between the two neighbors. In response to the escalation of border clashes between Azerbaijan and Armenia in July 2020,[31] the Spokesperson of Iranian Foreign Ministry Abbas Mousavi, announced that Iran was intent to reconcile the points of views between the two sides and lead mediation —once requested from the two waring countries to evade further escalation. Apparently, Iran has used a double-edged policy to deal with the two rivals. Some Armenian officials accused the Iranian government in 1994 of allowing six Azeri aircraft to use the airfield in Iranian Azerbaijan to strike Armenian targets in the Karabakh heights. One month later, a US newspaper claimed that an Iranian military officer was arrested in Karabakh.[32]

Map 1.2: Disputed Areas Between
Azerbaijan and Armenia

Source: Map used under license from Shutterstock.

During the most intense periods of war between Azeri and Armenian forces, Iran provided humanitarian aid to the refugees fleeing the disputed zone. Amid a visit to Iran, Irshad Aliy, the head of Azerbaijan's Committee for Refugees, expressed his gratitude to Iran in a statement. He said that Iran saved Azerbaijan from an inescapable crisis by housing 100,000 refugees from the Nagorno-Karabakh War. Similarly, Iran's Supreme Leader Ayatollah Ali Khamenei met with Azerbaijan's President Heydar Alirza Aliyev, declaring Armenia as the aggressor in Azeri territory.[33]

Despite the aforementioned developments, Azerbaijan remained relatively distrustful of Iran's close ties with Armenia. This adversely impacted relations between the two countries. In turn, some Iranian journalists accused Azerbaijan of aligning with both Iran's opponents at home and abroad and of participating in the US-Israeli campaign — which calls for isolating Iran and threatening its legitimate security and economic interests in the Caspian Sea region.[34]

In her book *Iran's Foreign Policy in the South Caucasus: Relations with Azerbaijan and Armenia*, Marzieh Kouhi-Esfahani, a lecturer at Durham University, criticizes reports published by the European Strategic Intelligence and Security Center, which reveal concerns over the support of Iran's Foreign Ministry for Armenia. The reports argue that the Iran–Armenia alliance serves Iran's hidden agenda, which threatens the "efforts undertaken by the international community to bring stability to the region and to achieve a peaceful settlement of the Nagorno-Karabakh conflict. They also warn "of Iran's will to use the Caucasus as a battlefield of a proxy war with the United States and the European Union in the framework of its nuclear program." Kouhi-Esfahani provides a pro-Iran justification arguing, "Iran has [....] tried to take a non-provocative, non-confrontational and pragmatic approach in the South Caucasus."[35]

The interference of other countries in this region like the United States, NATO or Israel — seeking to deploy their troops across Central Asia and the Caucasus region to serve their relative strategic interests — raises Iranian security concerns. The United States established military bases in Uzbekistan, Kyrgyzstan and Tajikistan as most Taliban and al-Qaeda leaders hid in the territories surrounding Afghanistan, particularly in southern Kyrgyzstan and Tajikistan. They later sneaked into Iran through the Afghan border; in return, Iran faced accusations of harboring them.

It is worth mentioning here that the fears of Islamist and radical terrorist ideologies led the US Congress to pay nearly $160 million to Uzbekistan for empowering it to fight against terrorism.[36] In response, former IRGC Commander General Rahim Safavi stressed that the expansion of NATO toward the East is a threat to Iran's national security, adding that Iran would exert all efforts possible to prevent any military cooperation between the Central Asian republics and the United States and would prevent them from joining NATO.[37] Iran, accordingly, concluded bilateral security treaties with the Central Asian republics.[38]

During former President Heydar Aliyev's tenure and amid the growing influence of the United States on Baku, Aliyev was pressured by Washington to distance himself from Tehran. When Ilham Aliyev succeeded his father as Azerbaijan's president, he generally pursued the same approach of his father toward Iran in the last years of his tenure. He established close ties with the West, particularly with the United States. Azerbaijan was also in alignment with Turkey, which is pro-US and a NATO member country.[39] Iran feared that NATO would get the upper hand in its strategic sphere of influence, given the fact that Baku sought to forge closer ties with the organization and secure membership.

Iran has criticized the growing relations between Azerbaijan and Israel. For Tehran, Israel's presence along its border is a threat to its national security. These Iranian concerns were explicitly apparent in March 1996; back then Iran's Foreign Minister Ali Akbar Velayati accused Azerbaijan during his visit to Baku of risking Iran's security by forging a strategic alliance with Israel.[40] Iran fears that the growing Azerbaijan-Israel alliance, given its military and intelligence dimensions, will contribute to destabilizing northern Iran — though the alliance is not official yet.

Iran-Azerbaijan tensions escalated after the Azeri security apparatus submitted a report to the Azeri government which described how Iran had enhanced its military buildup along the Azerbaijan border. Many Azeris are influenced by Iran; it has growing control over Shiite practices in the country, the report adds. According to official statistics, 22 out of 150 Shiite schools in Azerbaijan are completely under Iran's control. When Rouhani assumed office in 2013, official communication with these schools increased; more than 20 agreements were concluded with Iran's governmental sectors.[41]

US sanctions on Iran were lifted during Obama's administration in 2015; since then, cooperation expanded and a breakthrough was achieved. To reap the promising economic benefits in light of Iran's nuclear deal (JCPOA), Azerbaijan boosted ties with Tehran, which possesses 18 percent of the world's gas reserves. Azerbaijan could secure significant economic benefits by allowing Iran to establish gas pipelines through its territory to Europe. Their coordination strengthened further; President Ilham Aliyev visited Tehran in

2016 and met with Iran's Supreme Leader Ali Khamenei and President Hassan Rouhani.[42]

Considering the overall history of Iran-Azerbaijan relations, one can conclude that bilateral relations are witnessing gradual-consistent growth despite previous hurdles and mutual suspicions over relations with rival countries. The withdrawal of the Trump administration from the nuclear deal in May 2018 and the reimposition of sanctions on Iran limited economic cooperation and adversely impacted the longstanding stability of relations between the two sides.

In a nutshell, when Iran adopts its strategic vision toward Central Asia and the Caucasus countries, it takes into consideration their geopolitical significance and is fully aware of their massive natural resources. Consecutive Iranian governments have crafted plans and strategic objectives for the sake of maximizing the potential economic gains. Tehran, therefore, sought to enhance trade and political cooperation; contribute to establishing security and stability in the region, considering the danger arising from the region's ethnic struggles which may creep deep into Iran, or at least touch its border. Iran also aims to break the longstanding international isolation and reposition itself in the region as an influential power. Iran never overlooks the use of ideology as a soft power tool to materialize its strategic expansionist project, particularly through exploiting religion, culture, identity and nationalism. In its pragmatic foreign policy, Iran pays greater attention to economic and security objectives. Yet, it also uses religion, culture, race and language to mobilize internal forces and create considerable grassroots support. Iran accords greater priority to diminishing the interventions of foreign powers in the region, most prominently the United States, NATO and Israel.

Chapter Two

IRAN'S SOFT POWER TOOLS: CULTURE AND IDEOLOGY

Iran's Policy Toward the Region's Secular Governments

The peoples of Central Asia lived for 70 years under the Soviet Union. The post-Soviet governments maintained a grip over clerics and religious institutions, leading to the establishment of modern secular societies. These new governments never exploited Islam to legitimize their ruling systems despite the dominant role of Sunni Islam in some of them; therefore, they deemed Iran's Islamist discourse as a threat. Iran has been fully aware from the very beginning of their attitude, so it has seldom spoken up about exporting its 1979 revolution to the region. In fact, it also adopted a secular foreign policy approach toward them.

However, Iran's influence has still been effective, given its common history and identity with the region. Whenever possible, Iran has worked to penetrate deep into the region's culture to reshape its identity as it sought to craft a new identity after the fall of the Soviet Union. Iran sought to impose its Shiite identity instead of the region's growing Sunni identity — paving the way for building a conducive investment environment and effective relations that would positively reflect on its economy and ambitions to lead the region.

With its growing influence, Iran attempted to diminish the cultural influence of Sunni states, most prominently Saudi Arabia and Turkey. Iran was concerned that Saudi influence would expand across the Caucasus in the post-Soviet era as the peoples there are passionately connected to the two holiest cities in Islam — Makkah and Madinah — and to Sunni Islam which was suppressed during Soviet rule. Iran managed to an extent to make the Central Asian republics believe that their ultimate common challenge was to counter the "Salafist" currents from Saudi Arabia and the Arabian Peninsula — as it claimed.

Iran convinced the Central Asian republics to sign treaties to form an alliance to counter what it called "Salafism." Iran's diplomatic apparatus and the IRGC quietly leveraged this to sideline Sunni thought and open variant paths toward Shiite and Sufi beliefs. Iran's educational and religious institutions started to monopolize the Central Asian youth at the expense of Sunni ones.

Using diplomacy, Iran exploited Sufi leaders in the region such as Abusa'id Abolkhayr, Baha' al-Din Naqshband, Khawaja Yousif al-Hamadani, Najm al-Din Kabri and others to develop public trust. The writings of prominent Sufi scholars are in Persian (Farsi). Iran relied on the language to promote its religious heritage and penetrate deep into the culture and ideology of Central Asia amid the absence of official diplomacy by Sunni states.[43]

Iran will not impede the introduction of any Islamic current in this region — even if these are deemed nonconformist by the majority of Muslims. But it will resist Sunni Islam that is adopted in Arab countries, especially in Saudi Arabia. This is why Iran is concerned about the spread of Salafist theories and explicitly fights what it calls "fundamentalist Salafism/ Wahhabism" movements from the Indian subcontinent and the Arabian Gulf. These movements have significantly grown in Pakistan, Afghanistan, the Caucasus and Central Asia. Iran attempts to expand the scope of its contacts and intelligence apparatuses in Central Asia[44] to influence the collective consciousness of the Central Asian peoples and ensure that they embrace Khomeinist anti-Western rhetoric by criticizing the Western presence in their countries (the presence of the United States, Russia and Europe). The second goal of Iran, which is the most important, is to halt Sunni expansionism in the region.

Iran avoided explicitly promoting its revolutionary ideology and spreading it among all regional countries, given the differences in religious sects. Further, Iran is aware that the ruling elites in the region have embraced secular values, so they will not likely accept Iran's revolutionary ideology. Iran resorted to crafting a gradual pragmatic policy that does not take its Islamic revolutionary model as a bedrock, but rather a Persian pragmatic model is taken into consideration.[45] To achieve this end, Iran has never hesitated in supporting individuals or parties that align with its interests as well as empowering them to assume decision-making positions.

Limits of Iran's Soft Power

University Distinguished Service Professor, former Dean of the Kennedy School of Government at Harvard University and former Chair of the National Intelligence Council (1993 to 1994 during the Clinton administration) Joseph S. Nye argues that a country's power does not depend solely on its military power (hard power) but also on its soft power, which is an effective weapon to achieve goals through persuasion and attraction rather than coercion and payment. According to Nye, a country's soft power includes three main resources: "its culture (in places where it is attractive to others), its political values (when it lives up to them at home and abroad), and its foreign policies (when others see them as legitimate and having moral authority)."[46] Iran attempted to activate its soft power through its Shiite ideology, history and culture in Central Asia. The question to be raised here is, to what extent has Iran managed to use its soft power?

Iran's soft power has been quite effective, most prominently in Tajikistan; secondly, in Azerbaijan — elsewhere one cannot argue that it has had any tangible success. Tajikistan is a

Sunni majority country, yet Iran tried to penetrate it for the sake of some influence over its domestic affairs. In light of Iran's political ambitions, Tajikistan is of great significance due to a host of factors that contributed to the establishment of good ties between the two countries. First, both countries share a common identity; the dominance of Islam and the fact that most Tajiks are of Persian origin — compared to the rest of the Central Asian republics. Second, Persian culture and language are entrenched within Tajik society. Finally, the spread of sectarian tensions and the rising concerns of Persian-origin Tajiks about the dominance of Turkish-origin Tajiks over decision-making in the country has been exploited by Iran.

Most of Tajikistan's population fall into the Tajik ethnic group that shares a common history and culture with the Iranian people. This factor influenced Iran-Tajik relations. For years, Iran has been working to expand its influence in Tajikistan, exploiting its fragile economic situation, in addition to reviving Persian nationalistic sentiments among Tajiks.[47]

Between 1995 and 1998, Tajikistan's President Emomali Rahmon visited Tehran several times and concluded a host of agreements in the fields of culture, economy and defense. Iran hosted the UN-sponsored inter-Tajik talks between the Tajikistan government and representatives of the United Tajik Opposition (UTO) from 1996 to 1997. Until 2002, the two countries enjoyed good ties and accordingly concluded nine protocols for cooperation in the cultural, economic and political fields.[48]

Iran's charitable and cultural activities fall solely within the ambit of its religious institutions: The Imam Khomeini Relief Foundation, Al-Imam Al-Ridha Charity Foundation, Zahra Foundation Ltd., Iran's Cultural Center, Huda Global Library and Iran's Red Crescent. Iran cooperated with educational institutions in Tajikistan, inaugurating a branch of the Iranian Open University — deemed one of the most prominent Iranian educational projects in the country. Rafsanjani laid the foundation stone of the project and nearly 700,000 students are enrolled in the university. This happened after Iran had managed to penetrate the only Islamic university in Tajikistan. Taj al-Din Essamdinov, who graduated from Al-Mustafa International University (MIU) in Qom, was appointed as the university rector. As a result, 27 of the university staff were fired over accusations of links to Salafi groups and carrying out espionage activities for Saudi Arabia. Later, Iran replaced the educational curriculum in this Sunni university with other courses that are taught in Qom to transform the only Sunni university in Tajikistan into a Shiite one.[49]

Further, Iran supported some revolutionary parties to place pressure on the Central Asian republics that opposed its penetration into the region. This approach was similar to Iran's support for the Islamic Renaissance Party of Tajikistan. Founded in 1973, this party is based on the Muslim Brotherhood's thought process in terms of ideology, principles and objectives, and even though it is a Sunni party, Iran never hesitated from supporting it to achieve its ends. Iran has often denied its direct role in the armed internal conflict known as the Tajik Civil War (1992 to 1997), claiming it was a conflict between tribes, with no links to religion. "The state-TV channel of Tajikistan released a dangerous documentary of Iran's history in funding terrorism in Tajikistan and its involvement in many terrorist acts in the country since its independence, including training terrorists on arms, executing assassinations, and targeting security officials and intellectuals as well as implementing Iran's agenda inside Tajikistan...the Supreme Court in Tajikistan designated the Islamic Renaissance Party of Tajikistan as a terrorist organization."[50]

The leader of the Islamic Renaissance Party Mohy al-Din was invited to attend the 29th International Islamic Unity Conference in Tehran in December 2015. This invitation led to further tensions between the two countries given the fact that Mohy al-Din was received as a special guest for the conference and met Iranian Supreme Leader Ali Khamenei in Tehran. This represented a challenge for the Tajik government as did Iran's opposition to Tajikistan's enhanced relations with Saudi Arabia.[51] Iran was indirectly involved in toppling Rahmon Nabiyev in 1992, after which the civil war erupted.[52]

Although Iran achieved some success in terms of influence over Tajik cultural and religious fields, its influence has precipitously declined over the years; Dushanbe severed relations with Tehran. Upon an order by the Tajik authorities, Iran's embassy shut down in July 2017 as well as the offices of its trade and cultural representatives in northern Tajikistan. In addition, the publications of the founder of Iran's political system along with the publications of other Iranian clerics were banned. The Tajik authorities also ordered the closure of Iran's trade and cultural center in the northern Tajik city of Khujand.[53]

The secular political system implemented by the Rahmon government strongly contributed to stoking tensions between the two countries. Iran has been a source of concern and fear for the Tajik leadership because of its Shiite political system which differs significantly from Dushanbe's. This halted the strengthening of their relations, especially cultural cooperation; Iran promotes a sense of common culture and identity to penetrate societies.

The failure of the union of Persian-speaking countries which Ahmadinejad promoted clearly revealed the divergence in the two countries' views and political values as well as the ideological standoff between the two governments. Kazaz Mahdi Hafteh, professor of political science at Payame Noor University (PNU) in Tehran said, "The union of Persian-speaking countries never worked out due to the different political values; Iran and Afghanistan are Islamic countries whereas Tajikistan tilts toward Western values,"[54] adding that the ideological dilemma is one reason among others that weakened the Iran-Tajikistan relationship.

Azerbaijan is a top priority for Iran due to a host of considerations which impact its unity: common ethnicity and religion, nearly 6 million Azeris live in Iran of which 60 percent speak Persian and both countries share a border. Iran is concerned about the revival of the longstanding Azeri demand to be united as one people. Iran's behavior toward Azerbaijan has been marked by rejecting the longstanding proposal of uniting Greater Azerbaijan (also known as Whole Azerbaijan, see Map 2.1), entrenching sectarianism at the expense of nationalism and financing many cultural, social and political organizations in Azerbaijan. Tensions were exacerbated when the Azeri authorities accused Iran of working to impose its political model in Baku.[55]

Map 2.1: Greater Azerbaijan/ Whole Azerbaijan

Source: Scribble Maps. [56]

The aforementioned helps us identify the most prominent challenges facing Iran, particularly when crafting its soft power stratagem. Iran walks a tightrope between exploiting three main soft power tools: sectarianism, nationalism and pragmatism. Sometimes it resorts to giving up its main tools; sectarianism and nationalism and tilts toward absolute pragmatism when facing discontent and resistance from the countries that it targets.

As for Iranian leaders, their country has several disagreements with Azerbaijan: Baku is avowedly secular and hostile to the Shiite population in both countries. Although Baku and its outskirts are to a great extent secular, the population at large is still religious. Former Iranian Ambassador to Baku Ali-Reza Bigdeli noted, "Shiite Islam in Azerbaijan is a fact of life. There are forces in the country which do not want to acknowledge this fact. They do not want to admit that Islam has deep roots in Azerbaijan. Iran does not wish to focus on the strength of Shiite Islam among the majority of the Azeris, but we cannot remain silent when Islamic sensibilities are under constant attack by those who do not wish to see friendly relations between our two peoples."[57]

Further, Iran has condemned the presence of American Christian evangelical groups in Azerbaijan, and accused the United States of seeking to turn Azeris away from Islam. "Fundamentalist Christians proselytize using humanitarian front organizations in cities such as Baku and Lankaran," according to Iranian sources. Some unofficial "conservative" Iranian sources claimed that these organizations managed in the 1990s to convert 5,000 Azeris to various Christian evangelical sects by spending $15 million to indoctrinate Azeri Shiites.[58] The Iranian government decided to avoid, in general, any interference in the Azeri government's policies in relation to Islam; however, it is important here not to turn a blind eye to the significance of religion in Iran's stratagem toward Central Asia. The government of Azerbaijan exploited religion as a tool in its relations with Iran. For example, during Aliyev's presidency, the Azeri government on many occasions accused Iran of supporting the opposition, particularly during the 1998 presidential election. In December 2007, the Azeri Court for Grave Crimes sentenced 15 members of the opposition to lengthy prison terms for high treason and other crimes involving the passing of information to Tehran about the activities of Israel, the UK and the United States in Azerbaijan. In response, the Iranian government summoned the Azeri ambassador in Tehran and expressed its strong objection to this baseless accusation — as it claimed.[59]

Turkmenistan tops the list of Iran's ambitions in the region. Iran's first embassy in Central Asia was inaugurated in Turkmenistan's capital Ashgabat. To further deepen bilateral relations, especially in the economic and trade fields, Iran initiated in 1996 the establishment of the Mashhad-Sarakhs-Tajan railway track. At the first stage, the railway track was 165 kilometers starting from Fariman station near Iran's Mashhad and extending to the Sarakhs border. It was then connected to a 130-kilometer railway track stretching to Niyazov station in Ashgabat.[60]

Iran is highly interested in Turkmenistan for a host of reasons, namely: the long-shared border and for the fact that nearly 2 million Turkmens live in Iran, half of Turkmenistan's population. Yet the Turkmen community represents the same concern for Iran as the Azeris; Turkmenistan is a vital sphere of influence and a source of concern at the same time. Thus, Iran can use its Turkmen community as a bargaining chip with Ashgabat.[61] Moreover, the Turkmens and Iranians enjoy strong cultural bonds, probably because Turkmenistan had been part of Iranian territory in the past. Iran's national interests and foreign policy toward Turkmenistan are based on the following considerations: Turkmenistan's economic power, especially its abundance of oil and gas; its geographical location, standing as the gateway for Central Asia; and its membership in the ECO, a highly significant organization for Iran; and finally, it is among the Caspian littoral countries.[62]

Despite the previously mentioned pro-Iran variables in Turkmenistan, Tehran faces a host of obstacles to its ambitious projects in this country, most prominently: first, its secular political system despite its Muslim majority population. This constitutes a serious threat in the face of Iran's theocracy, which always exploits religion, particularly the Shiite sect, to influence the peoples and systems of other countries. Second, the strong influence and presence of the United States, Turkey and Israel in Turkmenistan.[63]

Kyrgyzstan is highly significant in Iran's strategy toward Central Asia as it is located between China and Tajikistan, neighboring Kazakhstan and Uzbekistan, and through which the Silk Road passes. Islamist fundamentalism was active in the western part of this country, particularly in the Fergana Valley. Later, Uzbekistan's Islamist movements operated in the Batken Region and the Pankisi Valley. It is believed that these Islamist movements were influenced by al-Qaeda and it was easy to identify their links with Iran. Yet, Kyrgyzstan has maintained notably good ties with Iran and has concluded many agreements in various fields.[64]

In Uzbekistan, Iran's ties have flourished since the collapse of the Soviet Union — thanks to the unique status of Persian culture in this country. Its two cities Samarkand and Bukhara are deemed the focal points of Persian culture in Central Asia —[65]

despite the significant decline in the use of the Persian language in favor of local and Russian languages in light of social, cultural and civilizational developments.

Every now and then, we witness discontent from the Central Asian republics over Iran's political activities in their territories; they are still wary of fully opening the door to Iran. They collaborated to counter its illegitimate polices. Uzbekistan and Tajikistan repeatedly accused Iran's covert apparatuses, variant religious groups and security and intelligence proxies of seeking to destabilize Central Asia's secular order.[66]

This is why the Twelver Shiite minority[1] is continuously repressed, remains isolated by the Azeris and Ironis in Samarkand and Bukhara and is viewed as an agent of Iranian influence.[67]

In a nutshell, we can conclude that Iran's soft power that rests solely on Shiism is still of limited influence in Central Asia for many reasons, namely: the effectiveness of Sunnism and secularism, the region's globalization and openness toward global cultures, its fears of Iranian revolutionary philosophy and principles after observing the sectarian ramifications of exporting Iran's revolution to the Arab world.

Exploitation of Cultural Heritage and Nationalistic Calculations

Iran presents itself as the overarching guardian and protector of Shiites across the world, emphasizing that its policies are governed by a set of values that transcend worldly interests or calculations. It also claims that religion, particularly Shiite jurisprudence, is the primary criteria that determines its options, meaning its policies. This jurisprudence propaganda

---

(1) Ja'afari (Twelver) Shiism is the official state religion in Iran, which roughly 75 percent to 90 percent of Iranians adhere to.

restarted following the renewed conflict between Armenia and Azerbaijan (the Second Nagorno-Karabakh War) in 2020. Since Iran always claims that its foreign policy rests on its religious values, it should have aligned with Azerbaijan whose population is 70 percent Shiite against Armenia whose majority is Orthodox Christian. Yet, since the outbreak of the First Nagorno-Karabakh War (1988–1994), which resulted in the deaths of 30,000 people, Iran has backed Armenia.[68]

Iranian support to Armenia does not stem from its belief in the latter's right to the disputed region of Nagorno-Karabakh whose majority is Armenian and is internationally recognized as part of Azerbaijan. Its backing of Armenia is merely due to its longstanding disagreement with Azerbaijan; Baku's exploitation of oil and gas in the Caspian Sea after World War II. Iran officially objected to Azerbaijan's recent agreements with foreign firms on oil exploitation in the Caspian Sea. In response, former Iranian President Hassan Rouhani was quoted as saying that his country enjoys warm and friendly relations with Armenia that set an exemplary model to the world. Iran's position, here, stems solely from its interests without considering its sect; this conflicts with the image it has been promoting in the Arab world, specifically within Arab Shiite communities and completely whitewashes all of its claims that it is committed to protecting Shiite interests.[69]

Using ideology as part of its soft power tool kit has proved to be fruitless; accordingly, Iran has sought to use nationalism, a tool that is much more apparent in employment than ideology. To maintain its cultural ties with the Central Asian republics, Iran has adhered to its common cultural-nationalistic legacy. The legacy of Persian supremacy that was left behind by the educational system of the Pahlavi shah is still effective and clearly represented in current textbooks to a great extent. The link of Iran to its past can be observed in traditional holidays such as Nowruz (Persian New Year) or Sizdah Be-dar (Nature Day). Both are derived from ancient Persian traditions and Zoroastrianism. The cultural bonds between Central Asia and Iran have strengthened their relations to some extent. Iran has entrenched its own cultural and nationalistic influences in Central Asia since its early history. Some Central Asian republics smoothly absorbed Persian and Iranian culture; many of the same holidays celebrated in Iran such as Nowruz are also official holidays in all of the Central Asian countries. In addition to their shared cultural and religious heritage, several cultural exchange programs were agreed between Iran and the Central Asian republics through which Tehran exported non-religious books, movies, journals, television and radio programs.[70] The table below highlights the most prominent ethnicities, languages and religions in Central Asia.

Table 2.1: The Most Salient Ethnicities,
Languages and Religions in Central Asia

Republic	Ethnicity	%	Language	%	Religion	%
Azerbaijan	Azeris	90	Azeri	89	Shiite Muslims	93.4
	Dagestanis	3.2	Russian	3	Orthodox Russians	2.5
	Armenians	2.3	NA	NA	A	2.3

	Armenia		Kazakhstan		Kyrgyzstan		
Ethnic group	Armenians	Azeris	Kazakhs	Russians	Kyrgyz	Russians	Uzbeks
	93	3	41.9	37	52.4	21.5	12.9
Language	Armenian	Russian	Kazakh (official)	Russian (communication)	Kyrgyz	Russian	Uzbek
	96	2					
Religion	Orthodox Armenians	Other religions	Muslims	Orthodox Russian	Muslims	Other religions	
	94	6	47	44	70	30	

Country	Ethnic group	%	Language	%	Religion	%
Uzbekistan	Uzbeks	71.4	Uzbek	74.3	Sunni Muslims	88
Uzbekistan	Russians	8.3	Russian	14.2	Eastern Orthodox	9
Tajikistan	Tajik	46.9	Tajik (official)		Sunni Muslims	80
Tajikistan			Russian		Ismaili and Shiite Muslims	10
Turkmenistan	Turkmens	73.3	Turkmen	72	Sunni Muslims	87
Turkmenistan	Russians	9.8	Russian	12	Eastern Orthodox	11

Data sources: Encarta and Universal (in French).[71]

Iran desires to establish cooperation with the region while reviving its forgotten Persian roots. To achieve this end, Iran sent specialized books and periodicals related to culture, literature and philosophy to the Central Asian republics and initiated academic exchange programs (through scholarships) with them.[72]

Iran has adopted a flexible policy toward Central Asia that has generated several opportunities to expand its influence in the future. Many Central Asians talk about Iranian intelligence activities across the region. Annually, Iran receives students from Central Asia and funds small Shiite groups. New Shiite movements — affiliated with Iran — emerged in Tajikistan. Iran also funded the establishment of many cultural centers and sought to establish Iranian studies departments at several universities operating under the supervision of Iranian embassies.

Iranian intelligence apparatuses actively operate in some Central Asian republics and support Shiite movements and parties to enhance Tehran's influence. They also established cultural centers to promote Iran's nationalist and sectarian ideologies. Iran does not provide any kind of funding and support without conditions; most prominently to promote its ideologies. Uzbek and Tajik authorities accused Iran's intelligence apparatuses of promoting Shiism and supporting and funding Shiite minorities to rebel against them and destabilize national security.[73]

Iran enjoys longstanding cultural bonds with Central Asia which basically stem from its 3,000-year role in this region. Against the backdrop of this historical legacy, Iran not only exploits religion but also other cultural and nationalistic factors such as common language and folklore. Iran's investment in its cultural legacy includes joint broadcast agreements and facilitating the participation of Iran-affiliated institutes in Central Asia and the Caucasus. Iran aims to strengthen its ties with both regions to create what is known as the "Greater Iran."[74]

Iran hopes that citizens of Iranian origin will help in boosting its ties with the regions. In the Caucasus, Azeris are culturally Iranians; they follow the Ja'fari (Twelver) Shiite sect that is embraced by the majority of Iranians and speak Persian in Azerbaijan's Talysh dialect. Ossetians, who live in the Republic of South Ossetia (bordering Georgia) and the North Ossetia–Alania Republic (bordering Russia) are Iranians and speak Persian. Though they are not of Iranian origin, Armenians have strong cultural bonds with Iran because they lived under the Persian Empire for a long time and 300,000 Iranians of Armenian origin contribute to maintaining Iran's ties with Armenia.[75]

Some argue that Iran's cultural bias is endorsed by many Iranian pundits who view themselves as representatives of a culture that is superior and of richer history than any other in the Middle East. This radical nationalism determined Iran's view toward Central Asia and the Caucasus, with the aim of establishing the "Greater Iran," (Greater Irân or Irān-e Bozorg) or at least to Central Asia, and more particularly to Azerbaijan. Pro-Iran nationalists object to Azeris and other Central Asian peoples having their own national history, dismissing it as fake or fabricated. [76]

When reviewing the perspective of the aforementioned radical nationalists, it seems that Iran's cultural approach is in response to Turanism,[1] the first rival political movement

---

(1) Turanism refers to a political and cultural movement that calls for the unity of all Turkic peoples because they are culturally, linguistically and ethnically related. Günay Göksu Özdoğan identifies Turanism as "The unity of the Magyars and the Finns as well as the Turkic people, and in that sense has the same meaning as Pan-Turanism." See Günay Göksu Özdoğan, "The Case of Racism-Turanism: Turkism During the Single-Party Period, 1931–1944. A "Radical Variant of Turkish Nationalism" (PhD diss., Bokaziçi University, 1990), 22.

in the region. The movement, which has been strengthened economically and culturally, calls for the establishment of "Greater Turkey" based on Turkish nationalism (pan-Turkism). The Central Asian republics are concerned about Iran's nationalistic tendencies as it had pronounced its claim to annex parts of the Caucasus (except for Georgia) at the Paris Peace Conference (1919–1920). Iran called for the annexation of Baku, Derbent, Shamakhi, Ganja and Yerevan, emphasizing that these cities must be restored because they were part of Persia and most of their inhabitants are Muslims with Persian roots — adding that they have an affinity with Persia in terms of history, geography, religion and culture and a considerable number of the inhabitants of these cities turned to the Iranian government to protect them when they expressed their desire to return to Iran.[77]

The separatist movements in Iranian provinces; East Azerbaijan Province and West Azerbaijan Province, are considered threats to the unity of the Iranian state and obstacles to its ideological and cultural efforts that aim to expand its influence inside Azerbaijan. Every now and then, Azeri officials and citizens highlight the unity of the historical lands of Azerbaijan. According to their perspective, South Azerbaijan, their land, which is located specifically in Iran's East Azerbaijan Province and West Azerbaijan Province, is occupied and now they live in North Azerbaijan, which is now known as Azerbaijan.[78]

The Southern Azerbaijan National Awakening Movement (SANAM) aka (GAMOH) hosted in 2013 a conference in Baku against Iran, calling for the annexation of Iranian Azerbaijan provinces. This conference incited fury among Iranians. The most prominent reaction to this conference was that of Hossein Shariatmadari, Khamenei's advisor and

Kayhan's managing editor, a conservative Iranian newspaper. In his article, Shariatmadari claimed that the people of Azerbaijan aspire to be part of Iran, adding that the Azeri people deem the establishment of an Islamic system — parallel to that in Iran–a priority. He also claimed that Iran could propose to Azerbaijan to hold a referendum on rejoining Iran after it had been separated by from Iran by Russia (during the Soviet Union era).[79]

Mansour Haghighatpour, who was back then the chairman of Iran's National Security and Foreign Policy Committee, made stronger remarks than that of Shariatmadari. He said that 17 cities in the Caspian region countries, including Baku (Azerbaijan's capital) aspire to return to Iran. The Iranian backlash reached official levels; Iran's Foreign Ministry called on the Azeri ambassador to Tehran and expressed its objection to the separatists' conference in Baku. Earlier in February 2012, Azeri lawmakers demanded at a parliamentary session to change the name of their country from "Azerbaijan" to "North Azerbaijan," and to conduct a legal review on the two historical treaties: the Treaty of Gulistan and the Treaty of Turkmenchay because they granted Russia and Iran control over Azeri territories. They called on to change the name to North Azerbaijan to place further pressure on Iran and because South Azerbaijan, which constitutes two thirds of Azerbaijan's historical land, is located in Iran.[80]

In a nutshell, Iran's efforts to enhance its religious and cultural ties with the Central Asian republics have not been successful. It can be stated that Iran's ideology not only failed to address the crises facing the Central Asian republics but also did not catalyze prosperity. Iran sought to employ economic cooperation and trade as a means to secure greater religious and cultural influence in the region.

Chapter Three

IRAN'S ECONOMIC AND TRADE TIES WITH CENTRAL ASIA AND THE SOUTH CAUCASUS

In 1992, Iran sought to revive the Economic Cooperation Organization (ECO), which was established in 1985 by Turkey, Iran and Pakistan as the successor organization to the Regional Cooperation for Development (RCD) that was established in 1965 by the aforementioned three countries. As for the ECO, Iran endeavored to make Azerbaijan, Turkmenistan, Uzbekistan, Kazakhstan and Kyrgyzstan members but refused to let in Armenia and Georgia despite their good ties. Iran's selection policy has evolved from its ambitions to reshape this Muslim-dominated geographical region. During the ECO summit hosted in Tehran in February 1992, Iranian leaders expressed hope that this organization would turn into a big Islamic market as member countries have a total population of 250 million Muslims and an area extending across 4 million square kilometers.[81]

Dispute Over Caspian Sea Resources

Before the collapse of the Soviet Union, the Caspian Sea dispute was between Moscow and Tehran, yet they both coordinated maritime navigation, fishing and the exploitation of sea resources by following the tenets of the Treaty of Commerce and Navigation signed in 1940. Against the backdrop of the Soviet Union's collapse, the dispute expanded and included new littoral states of this closed basin such as Russia, Azerbaijan, Turkmenistan and Kazakhstan. The Caspian Sea extends across nearly 1,200 kilometers, with an average width of 300 kilometers and a maximum depth of 1,023 meters. The significance of the Caspian Sea is not only limited to its security and strategic location, but it also possesses massive energy resources: gas and oil; 200 billion barrels of oil and gas reserves are estimated at nearly 200 trillion cubic feet (tcf), according to the US Energy Information Administration (EIA), (see Map 3.1). Needless to mention its fish and caviar resources.

(82) Thus, no wonder the five littoral states of the Caspian Sea participated in tough negotiations over six summits; the last of which was held in Ashgabat on June 29, 2022.(83)

Map 3.1: Caspian Sea Oil and Gas
Reserves and Infrastructure

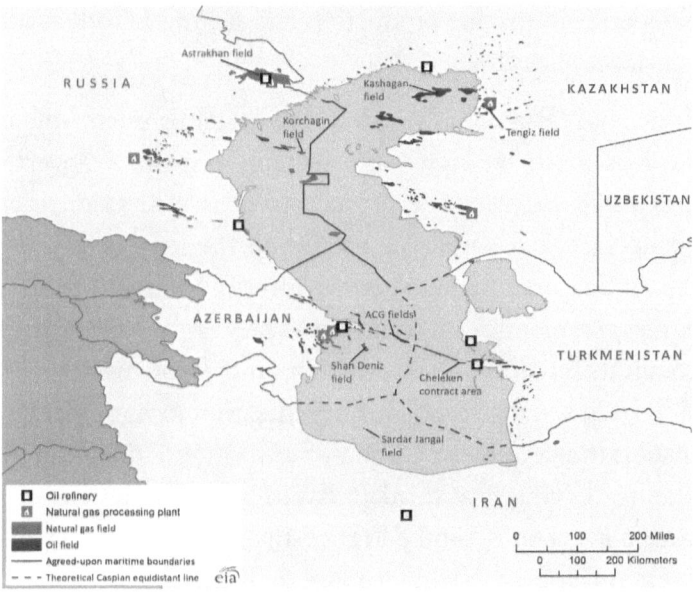

Source: US Energy Administration.(84)

Iran played an effective role in establishing the Caspian Sea Littoral States Cooperation Organization, which also includes Azerbaijan, Russia, Turkmenistan and Kazakhstan, with an aim to achieve the following:(85)

• Cooperate with the Caspian Sea littoral states in the exploitation of sea resources and in the fields of agriculture, energy and industry.

• Enhance regional security through economic cooperation.

• Cooperate in internal and external trade, especially in the oil and gas sectors.

• Cooperate in agriculture, especially in the items that will help the region to achieve self-sufficiency.

• Establish a wide land-sea transportation network, including gas pipelines.

• Cooperate in tourism.

• Cooperate in marine production and fishing as well as focus on caviar production.

Iran and Russia advocated the establishment of this organization to lay down the general principles governing the dealings between the littoral states as well as to reach a solution agreeable to all the parties on the legal status of the Caspian Sea, i.e., the legal convention. Iran aimed to defuse the disagreements that impacted the transportation of oil through its territory to the Arabian Gulf. Moreover, Moscow and Tehran sought to use this organization to monopolize oil transportation from the Caspian Sea to international markets without allowing any third party to intervene and reap the benefits. Further, it can be argued that Iran's call to establish this organization came in response to Turkey's call to establish the Organization of the Black Sea Economic Cooperation. Hence, one can infer that Iran's call for establishing this organization was based on security motives that are also related to its project of transporting oil through the Caspian Sea.[86]

The littoral states' disputes mainly revolved around the legal classification of the Caspian Sea as a locked lake or a sea. The legal classification also identifies resource distribution, sea division and the right to construct gas and oil pipelines on the seabed. If it is a sea, then it will fall under international maritime law and will be divided according to the coastline length. If it is a locked lake, its resources will be equally distributed between the five littoral states, each will receive a 20 percent share.

Iran demanded that the Caspian Sea be classified as a locked lake because its coastline accounts for a maximum of 11 percent of the sea while Azerbaijan and Kazakhstan wanted it to be classified as a sea, given their share in the coastline: Azerbaijan 23 percent, Kazakhstan 30 percent and Turkmenistan 17 percent (see Map 3.2).

Map 3.2: Defining the Caspian Sea: A Sea or a Locked Lake?

The debate about the legal status of the Caspian Sea-whether it is a lake or a sea-has been going on for more than 25 years. Here are examples of how maritime boundaries in the Caspian might be divided under each scenario:

SEA: The Law of the Sea uses the coastline and equidistant measurements to determine each country's exclusive economic zone.

LAKE: Each country would control 15 nautical miles from its shore for mineral exploration and another 10 nautical miles for fishing. Everything else would be shared jointly among all of the littoral countries

Source: Backgrounder. [87]

During the 1990s, Russia supported Iran in line with its political rather than economic interests. Moscow, back then, was seeking to win over the anti-US Iranian republic to its side. However, after 9/11, Washington's intentions to dominate the Caspian Sea became clearer, with it approaching Azerbaijan and Kazakhstan. As a result, Russia believed that from a strategic point of view, it was better to support both these countries to thwart the US move because by taking this step Moscow would not face any economic losses, neither would it lose Iran, which experienced escalating tensions with Washington and the West over its nuclear program.[88]

After difficult negotiations spanning over more than 20 years, the Convention on the Legal Status of the Caspian Sea was signed on August 12, 2018 by the presidents of the five littoral states (Russia, Iran, Kazakhstan, Azerbaijan and Turkmenistan), ending the dispute on the largest inland body of water in the world. The convention resolved the question over whether it is a sea or a locked lake, stating that it is a "sea" and granted it a "special legal status."[89]

The littoral states eventually agreed on several understandings, most prominently: the littoral states of the Caspian Sea shall not use their territories to undermine the security of each other; to jointly use the Caspian Sea waters while equally dividing up the seabed and underground resources according to international law; finally, when implementing major marine projects, the parties should carry out transportation, fishing, scientific exploration and pipelines according to agreed upon rules while taking into account appropriate measures to protect the environment.[90]

Though security, fishing and trade are among the agreed terms between the five littoral states, the establishment of energy transportation lines was not resolved. Iran seeks to gain the biggest share of transporting energy through the Caspian Sea. The longstanding dispute, especially between the southern littoral states (Iran, Azerbaijan and Turkmenistan) in relation to oil fields is still ongoing. On the contrary, Azerbaijan, Russia and Kazakhstan agreed on dividing the northern part of the Caspian Sea.

Iran was deemed the biggest loser in this convention; Iran possesses only 11 percent of the Caspian Sea coastlines, the agreement determined the division of the seabed and underground resources based on the aforementioned understanding between the five littoral states (according to international law) — despite the fact that the convention allowed the joint use of the sea waters (surface not the seabed). The convention, accordingly, sparked fury and discontent among Iranians at home against their government. Iranian officials and activists argued that concluding this agreement would relinquish their rights and risk the country's legitimate resources in the Caspian Sea because their government took this step to achieve one security objective; ensuring the absence of any foreign powers — especially the United States, which Iran views as the primary threat to its political system and national security — that undermine the security and stability of the littoral states of the Caspian Sea.

Iran only reaped a few benefits from the convention. This was reflected in the remarks of former Iranian President Hassan Rouhani, "The littoral states of the Caspian Sea managed to resolve 30 percent of its outstanding issues related to the sea after 20 years of negotiations. Other issues have remained unresolved and must be settled through dialogue and negotiations."[91] At the outset, Iran stressed on the equal division of the sea; to receive 20 percent of the sea, however, in accordance with the new convention its share would be nearly 14 percent of the seabed, compared to its coastlines.[92]

According to the Annual Strategic Report of the US National Security Council, the Caspian Sea dispute is likely to continue, adding that it is necessary to take Azerbaijan — given its location as a barrier between Iran and Russia — as a deployment center for US troops and naval and land bases. Washington exploited Iran's support to Armenia in its conflict with Azerbaijan and stoked up further disagreements between Iran and Azerbaijan. The United States invested nearly $20 billion in Azerbaijan's oil sector in the Caspian Sea and encouraged Baku to continue opposing Iran's demands regarding its share of Caspian Sea resources. As a result, Russia proposed its initiative before the five littoral states in which it called to ban the presence of foreign military forces in the Caspian Sea,[93] which is stipulated in the convention.

Iran's Project to Exploit Oil Resources in the Caspian Sea

Iran claims that its pipeline project in the Caspian Sea is more lucrative than any other pipeline project such as the US-Turkey one, and indeed it is. Tehran invests in its geographical location and pipeline infrastructure to promote this pipeline project. It seeks to establish a grip over oil resources in the Caspian Sea and be a key actor in transporting oil and gas from the sea to the rest of the world. Iran enjoys privileges in transporting oil and gas as it is strategically located between the Arabian Gulf and Caspian Sea. Iran's route is the most functional and economical in terms of transporting oil from this region to the world.

Iran is fully aware of its geopolitical privileges. In the north, it borders the Caspian Sea, Azerbaijan, Kazakhstan, Turkmenistan and Russia; therefore, it aspires to be the major transport route for Caspian Sea oil to the Arabian Gulf. If Iran managed to translate such ambitions into reality, the Arabian Gulf could face a serious backlash, given the fact that Caspian Sea oil reserves are equal to that of the former.[94]

The already established extensive pipeline infrastructure and oil terminals facilitate the transportation of oil to the Arabian Gulf. Needless to mention, the oil fields can be connected to Iranian oil refineries via pipelines, especially the oil fields in Azerbaijan, Kazakhstan and Turkmenistan. Such a process is feasible and does not cost much money when compared to the Baku–Tbilisi–Ceyhan pipeline. There are gas and oil pipelines in southern Azerbaijan connected to Iran's refineries in the north for the sake of addressing domestic demand.

Due to the aforementioned privileges, the Central Asian republics identified Iran as an outlet to develop and export their energy resources to the world whether via pipelines — circumventing Russia— or via Iranian oil and gas terminals (using oil tankers) because both transportation routes are much shorter than any other route.[95] Iran seized the opportunity by concluding a host of contracts for establishing gas pipelines that transport Central Asian oil to Europe via its territories. Iran managed to transport Turkmenistan's oil to Turkey and Europe through its territories, the shortest and cheapest route. Maritime transport plays a pivotal role in delivering crude oil from Azerbaijan, Kazakhstan and Turkmenistan via oil tankers to Iranian oil terminals on the Caspian Sea and is the most economically feasible option for transporting oil.

In light of the previously discussed privileges, Iran's project has another privilege as it only needs to connect certain existing pipelines (extending from South to North) to its refineries. Iranian researcher Mehrdad Mohsenin argues that Iran's pipeline is economically the most viable option for two reasons:[96]

• First, most of the infrastructure is already in place and Caspian Sea oil can be moved quickly and cheaply across Iran from its northern and central refineries which can handle considerable amounts of oil coming from the sea. Iran has four refineries in the north of the country which can exclusively handle Caspian Sea oil.

• Second, the Arabian Gulf is a good exit point from which most Asian markets can be served. Considerable amounts of Caspian Sea oil could be transported from Iran's terminal at Kharg Island which currently handles significant volumes of oil.

In the context of this project, Iran proposed two methods to transport Caspian Sea oil. Both methods are significantly cheaper than other pipeline routes. First, swap agreements are the cheapest method; and second, direct exports from northern to southern Iranian oil terminals.

The first option; swap arrangements with Iran, the oil would be transported from the Caspian Sea oil rich states: Azerbaijan, Kazakhstan and Turkmenistan to northern Iran. Iran then would deliver the same amount of oil to purchasers via its southern terminals in the Arabian Gulf; the revenues would then be collected for the three countries. Iran would benefit from this option given the fact that its oil fields are located in the south, so it would need to transport oil from the south of the country to its northern oil refineries, which handle 500,000-750,000 barrels of oil per day.[97]

To achieve this part of its Caspian Sea project, Iran's Ministry of Oil announced a three-stage plan. The first and second stages are carried out through swapping oil. The third stage is through direct oil exports to its southern terminals. For the first stage, Iran was keen to sign swap agreements with Kazakhstan and Turkmenistan so it can operate its northern oil refineries through establishing pipelines from Neka port in

Mazandaran Province, northern Iran. At this stage, Tehran and Tabriz's refineries will be able to handle 350,000 barrels of oil per day. It was planned in the second stage to transport 460,000 barrels of oil per day from the littoral states of the Caspian Sea to the Arak and Isfahan refineries through the existing pipelines. When this stage is achieved, Iran will be able to handle 500,000-810,000 barrels of crude oil per day through its northern refineries.[98]

The second method involves direct exports via existing pipelines, which is easier and cheaper compared to other pipeline projects. According to this method, Iran connects the oil fields in Azerbaijan, Turkmenistan and Kazakhstan via its existing pipelines which are also allocated for swap agreements. Iran, through this pipeline route, is aiming to transport 810,000 barrels of oil per day from the Caspian Sea directly to its southern terminals.[99] Iran also proposed to Azerbaijan to lay down a pipeline route from Bandar-e Anzali (Anzali port) in the western part of Gilan Province near Azerbaijan to reach ports on the Arabian Gulf. However, Baku and Tehran have not reached an agreement on this proposal.[100]

The overall amount of crude oil transported via Iran's proposed project is 162,000 barrels per day; half the amount will be delivered via swap agreements and the other half via the pipeline route from Neka port in the north to Tehran passing through Isfahan to the southern terminals. In May 1998, Iran announced the implementation of the first stage of the project; constructing a 392-kilometer pipeline from Neka port on the Caspian Sea to Tehran with a $400 million tender. In return, Iran charged a transit fee of $1.5-$2 per barrel. The Neka-Tehran pipeline had a transmission capacity of 250,000-300,000 barrels per day,[101] which could increase in the future.[102]

To refine greater amounts of Caspian Sea crude oil, Iran has sought to increase the capacity of its northern refineries in Arak, Isfahan, Tabriz and Tehran. If achieved, the transmission capacity of the Neka-Tehran pipeline would increase to 500,000 barrels per day. To achieve this end, the Iranian government allocated in 2003 nearly $500 million to upgrade the Tehran and Tabriz refineries to handle 370,000 barrels per day of high sulfur Caspian crude. This was followed by a $330 million tender to expand storage at Neka port and upgrade the Tehran and Tabriz refineries.[103]

The Iranian oil minister stressed that the Neka-Tehran pipeline is the best project to export Caspian oil. He said, "We believe that there is no other route [oil pipeline] which has the economic privileges of this route. The Baku–Tbilisi–Ceyhan (BTC) pipeline, which was extended on the floor of the Caspian Sea to deliver Kazakh and Turkmen oil, cost $3 billion whereas the initial cost of Iran's pipeline [project] is $300 million."[104]

In May 1996, Kazakh President Nursultan Nazarbayev signed a swap agreement with Iranian President Hashemi Rafsanjani to regulate crude swaps between the two countries through the Neka-Tehran pipeline. In line with the agreement, Kazakhstan transported 500,000 barrels of crude oil to northern Iran via Neka port in January 1997. In return, Iran transported the same amount of its oil to the Arabian Gulf while delivering the oil revenues to Kazakhstan.[105]

Considering the aforementioned, Iran worked hard to invest in its strategic location and existing oil industry infrastructure — the already established pipelines and refineries — so it could partake in the struggle for influence and be in a position to exercise greater clout in the region — through the existing Neka-Tehran pipeline and the proposed Bandar-Anzali-Tehran pipeline.

Economic influence, particularly through the pipeline project, is Iran's bedrock to integrate the Central Asian republics into its geopolitical, cultural and economic sphere. If Iran manages to operate this project while mitigating the effects of renewed US sanctions, it would be a leading country in the transportation of energy. This would positively reflect on Iran's comprehensive national power in the Middle East and prompt the Gulf states — given their capabilities in energy technology which exceeds that of Iran — to forge energy partnerships with the countries of Central Asia and the Southern Caucasus.

Trade Between Iran and Central Asia

Given the dire need to break the international isolation imposed by the United States, Iran has been expanding its economic and trade ties with the Central Asian nations by bolstering mutual relations with each country or forging regional alliances. Iran is greatly interested in Turkmenistan because of their shared border and Tajikistan in light of their common language and culture.

Though replete with resources, the Central Asian republics suffer from lagging development, which has helped Iran to play a leading role in developing their energy sector and securing a foothold in their markets, needless to say all the republics want to avoid Russia's development plans.[106] It is worth noting here that these republics, roughly speaking, view Iran as a country with a massive landmass, huge population, stable energy relations and good infrastructure. Yet, Iran's strategic location remains the most intriguing for them; Iran is the transit hub in the Eurasian continent from the East, West, North and South. This strategic location has been, over the course of history, a vital factor in Iran's economic relations and for boosting its trade. As a result of its strategic location, the Central Asian republics view Iran as a valuable partner as they are keen to find new ways to expand their trade and access the southern seas and the Mediterranean Sea.

Iran is fully aware that the markets of Central Asia and the South Caspian Sea are significant and promising for its goods, yet it is also aware of the fact that these markets, to be able to purchase Iranian goods, need to have sufficient liquidity, which is achievable by increasing their export revenues that is markedly dominated by oil sales. As previously mentioned, Iran proposed oil transportation projects to the Central Asian republics for them to sell oil in international markets.

The transportation deal that Iran aims to secure would involve the transportation of the region's oil through its own territory in return for Central Asian markets opening their doors to its goods. To achieve this end, Iran is constructing a land transportation network through which Central Asian trade passes through its territories. It is worth noting that this Iranian transportation network is likely to benefit from China's Belt and Road Initiative, as it inevitably passes through Iranian territories.

When comparing the current trade volume between Iran and the region to that during the Soviet era, we notice a tangible trade expansion; Central Asia and the Caspian region have become, to an extent, a significant market for Iranian exports. According to statistics, by the end of 2000, Iran's exports to all the Central Asian republics were worth $218 million and imports were worth $518 million. Azerbaijan, Armenia and Turkmenistan are Iran's major trading partners in the region.[107] Iran's trade relations with the region are still growing despite the hurdles and intense competition it faces with China and other countries.

Iran also signed various bilateral cooperation agreements with the Central Asian and Caspian nations and proposed multilateral measures involving the Caspian Sea littoral states. For example, in November 1992, Iran and Russia agreed to establish a joint research center for Caspian Sea studies. In February 1993, the Iran and Azerbaijan Joint Shipping Company inaugurated its ferry service between Iran's Anzali port to Azerbaijan's port in its capital Baku. Further, a host of bilateral agreements were signed between the Iranian Caspian provinces of Gilan and Mazandaran and territories in Azerbaijan and Turkmenistan.[108]

When Shavkat Mirziyoyev assumed office in December 2016 succeeding Islam Karimov in Uzbekistan, the country's relations with Iran notably improved; the two countries concluded a number of agreements. Pier Paolo Raimondi, a researcher in the Energy, Climate and Resources program at IAI, an Italian international relations think tank, commented on the concerns and fears of the former Uzbekistan president and the outcomes of the policy transformations adopted by the new president, " [A]t the beginning, President Karimov saw Iran as an Islamic-fundamentalist threat, fearing the proliferation of Islamist terrorist groups; therefore, he decided to limit its economic and political relations with the Iranian regime. The new Uzbek President Mirziyoyev expressed his intention to change track in an effort to improve the country's relations with its neighbors. Therefore, recently the two countries affirmed that they are working for increasing the trade volume from $400 million to $1 billion in the next few years."[109]

As a result, by the end of 2018, the trade volume between the two countries was valued at nearly $306 million; Uzbekistan's exports to Iran amounted to $172 million whereas Iran's exports reached $133 million. Now, there are nearly 120 joint projects by Iranian investors in Uzbekistan.[110]

In light of the above, Iran's northern provinces have become increasingly significant. Following the Soviet Union's collapse, the independence of Azerbaijan, Turkmenistan and Armenia facilitated communication between the peoples and officials of the new republics and the northern Iranian provinces. Due to this new reality, Iran's northern provinces became more significant when compared to the rest of the provinces in the country.[111] With the Iranian government giving them special attention, Iran's northern provinces witnessed accelerated economic growth compared to the others.

In 1991, the Iranian government's policy to develop the northern provinces was apparent. Iran concluded agreements with Azerbaijan and Turkmenistan to open new border ports in Iran's Eastern Azerbaijan Province, Western Azerbaijan Province and Mazandaran Province so that the citizens of these provinces could work in Azerbaijan, Kazakhstan, Turkmenistan and Armenia. The same effort was exerted toward Iran's Gilan and Khorasan provinces bordering Turkmenistan. Relations between the Iranian provinces and the Central Asian republics improved to the extent that the Anzali Free Zone was proposed during talks between the representatives of Gilan Province and Azerbaijan. In addition, Iran concluded trade agreements with Kazakhstan and Turkmenistan valued at $40 million.[112]

The Iranian pipelines would help in supporting trade with these republics and enhance job opportunities for many Iranians, especially in the northern provinces through which the pipelines would pass. This in addition to creating job opportunities for Iranians working in the Central Asian republics, which would witness prosperity because of the inflow of oil revenues. If Iran manages to implement its oil pipeline projects, it will gain a significant share of these oil revenues. Iran can forge further rapprochement with the Central Asian republics in other industries, with Iranians notably skilled in areas such as hydroelectric power, minerals, agro-processing, textiles and automobiles.

Tehran's international isolation has been very costly for the Central Asian republics; they have been unable to reap the full benefits of Iran's strategic location. Despite Iran being geographically connected to Central Asia through Turkmenistan, trade is still limited and sometimes witnesses a decline. For example, in the early 1990s, Iranian goods were exported to Central Asian markets but could not compete with Chinese products. By the end of 2012, Iran's trade volume with the region hit rock bottom, accounting for less than 3 percent of Central Asia's trade.[113] Thus, an important question that arises here is: have the consecutive US sanctions imposed on Iran since Washington's withdrawal from the JCPOA, negatively impacted its economic relations with the Central Asian republics?

Raimondi confirmed that Iran faces several challenges in its trade relations with the Central Asian republics as their foreign policy is based on avoiding backlash in response to circumventing US sanctions. He said, "In the economic sphere, Iran has to face some difficulties because of the foreign policy implemented by the CARs [Central Asian Republics]. Indeed, although CARs pursue a 'multi-vector' policy, they pay attention in particular to maintaining positive relations with other external players in their domestic context. Therefore, they are reluctant to engage with Iran if this would mean being affected by American sanctions."[114]

Over the past decades, the Iranian government has acknowledged the serious demands of the Iranian-Azeri community. In 1993, for example, Tehran recognized the new Ardabil Province as the third province in Iranian Azerbaijan, after the Western and Eastern Azerbaijan provinces. H. E. Chehabi, a scholar of Iranian studies at Boston University, argues that the Azeris' exploitation of Ardabil's social, political and cultural resources along with the collapse of the

Soviet Union allowed them to demand Tehran to grant them their long-awaited wish; Ardabil Province. [115] The Iranian government also invested considerable funds for developing infrastructure projects in the Azerbaijan provinces as well as between the Iranian-Azerbaijan provinces and Azerbaijan. As the Azerbaijan provinces are Iran's richest agricultural areas, Tehran has heavily invested in irrigation, which is vital for agricultural productivity. [116]

Further, Iran developed its border regions with Azerbaijan. For example, in February 2006, a new inter-modal hub on the Iran-Azerbaijan border was launched to provide an alternative route to long- trucking or rail routes around the Caspian Sea region. Rail freight can now reach its final terminal at Astara, the Iranian-Azeri border city, from Western Europe. [117]

Iran's trade with Azerbaijan is relatively considerable; exceeding the volume between Baku and Washington, despite the fact that the United States has placed pressure on Baku so that it aligns with its side against Tehran. However, Azerbaijan's trade relations with Iran declined in comparison to Europe. We notice a sharp decline in the percentage of Azerbaijan's exports to Iran in comparison to Azeri imports, which also gradually decreased. This blatantly contradicts the remarks of Iranian and Azeri officials, who have overstated the level of their bilateral trade relations. [118]

A statistical study on non-oil export capacities of Iran compares its exports to five neighboring countries: Azerbaijan, Armenia, Iraq, Turkey and Russia during 2005-2015. It concludes, based on four criteria: exports, export potential, unused export capacity and unused capacity of export potential, that the percentage of Iran's unused capacity to Azerbaijan is 80.1 percent and its unused capacity to Armenia is 58.8 percent (see Table 3.1). [119]

Table 3.1: Non-oil Export Potential of Iran to the Countries of the Region (2011-2015)

Country	Iran's available export to region 2 countries	Iran potential export to countries region 2	Unused export capacity	Unused export potential percentage
Turkey	1194	5032	3837	
Azerbaijan	143	752	609	80.1
Russia	239	692	453	65.4
Armenia	84	204	120	58.8
Iraq	5830	15,521	9691	62.1

Source: Scientific Research Publishing.[120]
Note: Figures are in millions of dollars and percent.

International North–South Transport Corridor

The promising rewards Iran is eager to reap from forging good ties with the Central Asian nations are: trade opportunities and employing this region to exit the international isolation that it suffers from. Iran also aims to invest in its strategic location to stand as a trading hub between the Caucasus and the Arabian Gulf and the rest of the world.

In the post-Soviet era, a wave of transregionalism boomed; many transregional (transboundary projects) were proposed by the countries that lie within the same geographical sphere and share common interests — with an aim to expand and deepen their partnerships. This was to be achieved by lifting tangible obstacles to trade; opening transregional trading routes over land and sea; and establishing free zones. The most significant transregional projects are the International North–South Transport Corridor (INSTC) and China's BRI which was proposed by China's president in 2013.

Though the two corridors overlap, in this book we mainly review the INSTC. Following the collapse of the Soviet Union, Iran proposed projects to expand its political and economic cooperation, facilitate transregional trade and establish land and sea routes connecting Asia and the Caucasus either by cooperation or competition with China, Russia and India. Among the projects proposed, the INSTC remains the most prominent. India, Russia, Central Asia and the Caspian nations have vital interests in this corridor, yet Iran plays a pivotal role by virtue of its geostrategic location at the intersection of the corridor.

The concept for establishing the INSTC was first laid down in 1993; however, the three countries: Russia, Iran and India did not, back then, sign an agreement regulating the transportation of goods through this new corridor until 2000. All parties ratified the agreement in 2002. Three years later, in 2005, Azerbaijan signed the agreement. Since then, 10 more countries have joined the project: Armenia, Russia, Belarus, Kazakhstan, Kyrgyzstan, Oman, Syria, Turkey, Ukraine and Bulgaria (observer).[121]

The bedrock of the INSTC is to deepen and expand interregional trade in South Asia, the Arabian Gulf and Northern Europe through an integrated network of rail, land and sea routes. The corridor is also meant to decrease interregional barriers to trade, especially those related to shipping costs and durations. In addition to having shared interests with INSTC member states, Iran is strongly committed to the project because of its own vital interests, namely: its aim to be the interregional hub for this geographical area and consequently reap the potential economic revenues from being a transit hub, in addition to deepening relations with the Central Asian republics.[122]

The most significant Iranian goal is to create more shared interests with a growing pool of regional and global powers, so that they can defend Iran's interests against the backdrop of international sanctions and counter-moves (the West and the Arabian Gulf). This goal was apparent when Iran proposed to link the Caspian Sea to the Arabian Gulf or the Indian Ocean through its territories via this corridor.

The comprehensive objective of the corridor is to expand interregional trade between the countries and regions that lie within the corridor's reach through decreasing trade costs and shipping durations. Studies of proposed corridor routes have concluded that they will reduce trade costs by about 30 percent and voyage time by 40 percent compared to traditional routes.[123]

The legal policy framework of the corridor was crafted in 2000 and the agreement was left open for other countries to join. The Ashgabat Agreement (an international transport and transit corridor facilitating the transportation of goods between Central Asia and the Arabian Gulf) is a legal framework that complements the INSTC agreement. The Ashgabat Agreement was signed by Oman, Iran Turkmenistan and Uzbekistan in 2011.[124] Later in 2016, Kazakhstan and Pakistan joined the agreement and India joined in February 2018.

After Pakistan and India joined the agreement, its geographical scope expanded to include South Asia in addition to Central Asia and the Arabian Gulf. The signatories to this agreement, while depending on Iranian and Omani ports, aim to improve transregional interlinkages to streamline the trade and transportation of goods and energy between Central Asia and the Arabian Gulf.

There are many Iranian motives behind the attempts to revive the INSTC. It provides a significant opportunity to integrate Iran's economy into the global economy, deepen national economic integration (trade, oil and service sectors) as well as boost interregional integration with vital destinations: Russia,

China, Central Asia and Europe. Boosting and expanding interregional economic integration will result in global interest in Iran's economy, hence global actors will want to avert Iran's isolation via sanctions and other restrictions. Iran wants to make sure that the imposition of sanctions on its economy is not an easy process. Interregional economic integration based on the existence of a connecting network to transport goods and energy, and one that is financially lucrative, will make the imposition of sanctions on Iran extremely difficult. [125]

It is clear that Iran is aiming to be a strategic hub (a point of intersection) for trade and transport routes between Central Asia, South Asia, the Arabian Gulf, Northern Europe and the Caucasus. To achieve this end, Iran is exploiting India's interest in accessing Central Asian markets and energy supplies while attempting to avoid passing through Pakistan's territories as much as possible. This is why India joined the INSTC, participated in developing Chabahar port and later signed the Ashgabat Agreement. The Central Asian republics are also interested in creating more opportunities to access energy markets, especially in South Asia, so that they lessen their dependence on Russian ports. As for Moscow, it is seeking to enhance its opportunities to access warm waters, needless to mention its shared interest with the INSTC participants to reduce tangible trade barriers. [126]

The development of Chabahar port is expected to provide Iran access to markets in Central Asia and Afghanistan, increase its oil and non-oil exports and help it achieve its other economic and political objectives. India, via this strategic port, will be able to send its imports to Afghanistan through Iran, thereby avoiding Pakistan, with which it has infamously contentious relations, and compete with China in spreading its influence in Central Asia. As for landlocked Afghanistan, the INSTC grants it access to the Indian Ocean; delivering its exports to India through Iran and thereby avoiding Pakistan's Karachi port.

The INSTC is a 7,200-kilometer-long multi-mode network of ship, rail and road routes. It is a cheaper and shorter alternative to the traditional (standard) route via the Suez Canal, (see Map 3.3). The Suez Canal will undoubtedly be affected when it is operational because it is 30 percent cheaper and 40 percent shorter than the traditional route via the Suez Canal. For example, shipments from Mumbai to Moscow would be delivered within 20 days and the annual transport volume of the INSTC is estimated to be between 20 million and 30 million tons of goods.[127]

Map 3.3: INSTC vs Standard Route (via the Suez Canal)

Source: Map used under license from Shutterstock.

India proposed to develop Chabahar port, located in southeast Iran and also financed by China, as an alternative to Pakistan's Gwadar port. New Delhi has invested $20 billion to develop this port as a trade project to access Central Asia's markets and connect with Afghanistan, hence bypassing Pakistan. Chabahar port is located on the Gulf of Oman and is 900 kilometers away from Afghanistan. In 2003, India concluded an agreement with Iran to develop the port, but the sanctions imposed on Iran have hindered the pace of its implementation. Apparently, India is anxious to get this port project completed to break the Pakistan-China stranglehold over its northwest frontier (see Map 3.4). [128]

Map 3.4: Iran's Chabahar Port and the China-Pakistan Economic Corridor (CPEC)

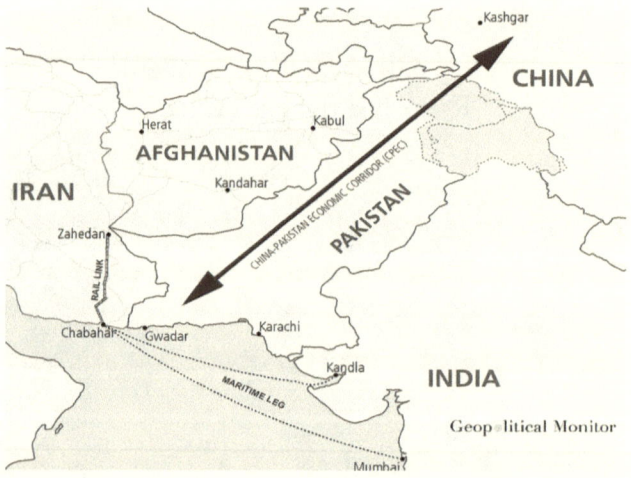

Source: Geopolitical Monitor. [129]

India aims to transport goods by sea from Jawaharlal Nehru port and Kandla port on the west coast of India to Bandar Abbas on the southern coast of Iran, then via land route shipments that are transported to Iran's Bandar-e Anzali port on the Caspian Sea. Eventually, the shipments would be delivered via a Russian rail net work to Russia and Europe. [130]

In 2014, three test shipments were carried out to examine the efficiency and feasibility of the INSTC. According to these tests, the new route was cheaper by 30 percent and the voyage time was shorter by 40 percent compared to the current all-sea route. The new route would reduce voyage time to nearly 18 days, i.e., half of the voyage time of the all-sea route.[131]

The first phase of Chabahar port was inaugurated in 2018. According to statistics, the load capacity of the port would increase to 9 million tons; it barely reached 3 million tons before its development. The port capacity is expected to exceed 80 million tons when the fourth phase is completed. Iran hoped that by the end of 2019 the port would have been operational despite the resumption of sanctions in 2018.[132]

To contribute to the India-led project that would also help in rebuilding Afghanistan's economy, the United States granted sanctions waivers for the development of Chabahar port and allowed the establishment of a rail route from Chabahar port to Afghanistan. This was done to help the war-torn Afghan government import unsanctioned goods such as medicine and food items via Chabahar port. "This [sanctions] exception relates to reconstruction assistance and economic development for Afghanistan. These activities are vital for the ongoing support of Afghanistan's growth," a US State Department spokesperson said in a statement.[133] Through the sanctions waivers, Afghanistan was given the green light by Washington to deal with Iran to import much-needed medicines and goods. This helped India to access Afghanistan's markets as well. Thus, through this port, Afghanistan has an opportunity to boost its ties with India and other regional powers.

Developments in July 2020 hindered the completion of the project and curbed the desired economic gains and the enhancement of trade and political partnerships between the parties involved. It was consecutively reported that India withdrew from a mega project that aimed to improve the railway connecting Chabahar and Zahedan in eastern Iran. According to some reports, Iran excluded India from the project against the backdrop of New Delhi's delay in commencing the project and hindering its funding. Other reports justified New Delhi's delay in funding the project because equipment suppliers and operators refused to participate in projects related to the railway construction due to their concerns that they would be targeted by US sanctions imposed on Iran. Interestingly, the aforementioned developments coincided with leaks about serious negotiations between Iran and China regarding the conclusion of a 25-year strategic partnership, which includes comprehensive security and investment. This partnership undermines India's partnership plans and cooperation opportunities with Iran.

Even if Iran and India resolve their disagreements and return to their agreement, given their desire to accelerate its implementation of the project, some obstacles still remain which may hinder its completion, namely: high construction costs, long distance, rough terrain and environmental degradation. Further, the US administration withdrew from the JCPOA in 2018 and imposed harsh sanctions on Iran. If the US sanctions regime against Iran expands and includs the INSTC, then, without a shadow of a doubt, Washington's opposition will impact Tehran's ability to manage the implementation of the rest of the project's phases in the Central Asian and Caspian nations unless the governments in these regions manage to reach some sort of understanding and agreement with Washington to receive sanctions waivers for the INSTC, which will not be an easy task.

Chapter Four

COUNTRIES COMPETING WITH IRAN FOR INFLUENCE IN CENTRAL ASIA AND THE CAUCASUS

The Central Asia and Caucasus region is a land of opportunity and great risk. It is a region of promising opportunities for Iran but at the same time is a threat to Russia, which is concerned about Iran's influence in this vital region. Russia aims to thwart the influence of Iran's theocratic model of governance in this region. Israel, on the other hand, is looking to secure a foothold in this region to be closer to Iran so that it is able to contain its influence and counter its nuclear project. As for the United States, it aims to deter Iran's creeping political and economic influence, noting that Central Asia and the Caucasus represent the gateway for China and India to play a greater role in this region. As part of its comprehensive regional confrontation with Iran, Saudi Arabia transferred its confrontation to this region, where it has entrenched its influence and boosted its cooperation with the Central Asian republics to avoid turning this region into an open sphere of influence for Iran.

Russia

This region does not generate opportunities exclusively for Iran. It is also of vital economic and political significance for Russia which shares historic bonds with a number of Central Asian republics. Russia has been concerned about Iran's influence in this region and has always viewed Iran as the biggest threat to the region, given its shared border. Iran is fully aware that Russia is a stronger state in all aspects as Iran is still listed as a developing country. Russia has been an effective factor in relation to Iran's policy toward the Arab world; Tehran has never deployed its regular army (Artesh) outside its national territory, fearing Russia's exploitation of the army's power vacuum inside its territory.

Iran's historical dynamic with Russia has created a longstanding complex in the psyche of Iranians that the

Russians have always sought to dominate their country. Following WWII, Soviet forces directly crept toward the north of Iran; they occupied it and the Soviet Union refused to withdraw until the UN Security Council pressured it to expel its forces. This was enough to create a longstanding deep fear of potential Soviet occupation in the minds of Iranians.

Even after the collapse of the Soviet Union, Russia still viewed Central Asia as its vital sphere of influence, the borders of the newly independent republics turned into its own security borders. Moscow has employed variant tools to increase its influence, military presence and dominance over Central Asian energy markets. Given this importance to Russia, it exaggerates the threats facing Central Asia from what it calls "terrorist groups" and ethnic tensions, claiming there are foreign countries that are intervening and supporting radicalism and sectarianism there; thus, it has been forced to coordinate with Iran in the context of addressing these fears.

But what actually pushed Russia to coordinate with Iran was its security concerns and common interests. For example, it coordinated with Iran in Afghanistan where both Moscow and Tehran worked together to fill the power vacuum left by the United States and in the aftermath of Europe's partial withdrawal and restructured political and security arrangements in the country for the sake of their interests.

For Russia, Central Asia is the geopolitical variable and the key gateway to controlling the world. It is well known that Russia's foreign policy toward the Central Asian republics is based on safeguarding its standing as a great power in the region — as mentioned earlier, Russia views their borders as a security buffer. Until now, Russia is playing a key role in this region; six post-Soviet republics engage in routine military drills led by Russia on their shared borders under the Collective Security Treaty Organization (CSTO).

The emergence of radical groups and growing competition between regional powers in this region, especially between Russia and Turkey, led Russia to maintain bases in four Central Asian republics: Tajikistan, Kazakhstan, Kyrgyzstan and Turkmenistan. This Russian move is also in the context of the international competition to militarize Central Asia.[134]

To better understand Russia's interests in this region, one must consider economic and military factors. The economies of the Central Asian republics are greatly connected to Russia's economy. In both exports and imports, Russia occupies a high rank in these republics. Needless to say, taking control of Central Asia's resources allows dominance over oil, gas, mineral and agricultural supplies from the region to Russia, China, the Indian subcontinent and the EU. This region enjoys tremendous oil reserves in addition to natural gas, oil, coal and other natural wealth. For example, Tajikistan has huge uranium mines that were discovered in the 1930s.

As part of Russia's cultural, educational, and scientific cooperation with the region the Moscow State University (MSU) and the National University of Science and Technology (MISiS) were opened in Dushanbe, Tajikistan's capital — where 5,000 Tajiks study. By the end of 2010, about 4,500 students had been registered in the Russian-Tajik Slavonic University (RTSU), Dushanbe.

Against the backdrop of Russia's entrenched influence in this region, Iran faces serious challenges in expanding its influence, given the fact that its pollical, economic and security interests are very often intertwined with those of Russia. Iran attempts to attract the Central Asian republics and enhance relations with them, yet this raises Russia's concerns as it views these republics as part of its own security and strategic sphere. Iran and Russia sometimes coordinate efforts to tackle crises, yet this is not necessarily reflected in their policies toward Central Asia.

At the military level, Russia works to disarm the Central Asian republics of nuclear weapons left from the Soviet Union's arsenal and attempts, using all possible means, to prevent nuclear weapons development in these republics.

Historically, Central Asia has been an arena of conflict between Russia and Iran. Tajikistan was never excluded from this conflict as it has been part of military alliances and economic blocs dominated by Russia. It joined the Eurasian Economic Community (EAEC or EurAsEC), the CSTO and the SCO, which are all dominated by Russia. Russia and Tajikistan signed an agreement extending the former's lease on Base-201 in Tajikistan until 2042. According to the agreement, Russia will provide Tajikistan with military and technical equipment.

Over the past years, Russia never allowed Iran to exclusively deal with Tajikistan; it has always been strongly present in Tajikistan. Russia is concerned that these Islamic republics may turn into theocratic states that adopt policies risking its vital interests in Central Asia as Iran does.[135]

In April 2015, the CSTO announced its plan to form a collective rapid deployment force to be stationed in Tajikistan to counter the invasion of Islamist militants. In 2017, Tajikistan received the first batch of Russian arms and equipment including T-72B1 tanks, BTR-80, BTR-70 armored personnel carriers, BMP-2 amphibious infantry fighting vehicles, Mi-24 and Mi-8 helicopters and D-30 howitzers. The batch also included anti-aircraft weapons, land surveying equipment, spare parts for armored vehicles, communication and administrative devices and a host of light weapons. The supplied armaments and military equipment to Tajikistan totaled $122 million.[136]

The United States

Since the 1979 Iranian revolution, enmity has marked and overshadowed Washington-Tehran relations. The United States views Iran's ruling system as a threat to its interests, especially in the countries neighboring Iran. Based on its concerns, Washington adopted an approach of sanctions and isolation to place pressure on the Iranian ruling system; to change it or at least change its behavior. On the other side, since 1979, Iran has deemed the United States as the major culprit of all the crises surrounding it. Without a doubt, following the collapse of the Soviet Union, the US presence in Central Asia meant Iran was encircled on its northern frontier. During its rearrangements in the region following the collapse of the Eastern Bloc, the United States managed to develop relations with the newly independent Central Asian republics and establish a presence on Iranian borders. With the passage of time, the US presence was enhanced further, especially after the US invasion of Afghanistan in 2001and in the context of the War on Terror (officially known as the Global War on Terrorism 2001-2021).

The climax of US moves against Iran in the region were during the years between 1991 and 1993. The US anti-Iran policy, back then, can be summarized as follows:

• The United States depicted Iran as a country that sought to promote Islamic fundamentalism. During his tour to Central Asia and the Caucasus in 1992, former US Secretary of State James Baker emphasized that the newly independent republics must avoid any cooperation with Iran.

• The United States disclosed that Iran's plans — benefitting from the collapse of the Soviet Union — were mainly to access the technology to develop an atomic bomb.

• The United States pushed the view that Iran hindered international peace efforts to resolve the Nagorno-Karabakh conflict between Azerbaijan and Armenia.[137]

Iran's concerns grew as the region was and is highly significant in the US strategy. Central Asia was identified as the key gateway for US hegemony in Eurasia — Washington formed new military, economic and security arrangements in the region. Tajikistan was the first country in Central Asia to sign a transit agreement with NATO for the International Security Assistance Force (ISAF) mission in Afghanistan. Oil has been the primary motivation in relation to the United States' moves in Central Asia as it is rich with tremendous oil reserves. The United States aimed to take control of oil fields in Central Asia and the Caucasus.

The strong US presence in this region, especially at its heart; Tajikistan, aimed to contain China's rising influence there. Washington structured geopolitical arrangements in Central Asia to curb China's strategic expansion on its western frontier as well as to prevent Russia from returning to its southern backyard; to isolate Russia from its historical spheres of influence; the Central Asian republics, a legacy of the Soviet Union. The US presence was also part of Washington's policy to isolate Iran and deprive it of the advantages arising from its geopolitical location, as it is connected to Central Asia on its northeastern frontier.

By exploiting the so-called US-led counterterrorism campaign, Washington entrenched its military presence in the region. It concluded a number of agreements to establish military bases in the Central Asian republics: Uzbekistan, Kyrgyzstan and Tajikistan and provided them with arms and training — to boost its presence and influence, so it could launch oil and gas projects that met its energy demands.

It launched the "energy project of the century;" the Baku-Tbilisi-Ceyhan (BTC) pipeline to transmit oil from the Caspian Sea through Georgia to Turkey's Ceyhan port on the Mediterranean Sea and then to the Atlantic area. Washington viewed this pipeline as a lifesaver; through which it could liberate itself from its crippling absolute dependence on Gulf oil and eliminate the longstanding Russian dominance over crude oil supplies from the Caspian Sea — which would eventually diminish Moscow's political and economic influence. The pipeline would help Washington corner Iran on its northeastern border, paving the way to force it to surrender to its control. This is in addition to preventing the transportation of materials, technology and expertise from Central Asia, namely Kazakhstan and Uzbekistan, for the sake of developing nuclear, conventional or beyond-conventional weapons — inherited from the Soviet Union — to rogue countries like Iran.

During the US occupation of Afghanistan, Iran cooperated with the United States to expel the Taliban as it was a source of concern. Tehran's condition to Washington was that the first president in the post-Taliban Afghanistan would have to be Shiite; the condition was met and the same went for Iraq.[138] Later on, the United States confronted Iran's role in Central Asia and curbed its economic and trade ties in the region. It was working to corner Iran at its northeastern frontier after having cornered it on its western border, the Arabian Gulf. Not only this, but the United States also aimed to deprive Iran of its strategic bargaining chip; the transportation of energy supplies as it offers the cheapest and shortest route to transit Central Asian and Caspian Sea oil.

China

With the greatest level of investment in this region, China has the most interests in Central Asia; especially after the majority of the Central Asian republics joined the SCO. In Central Asia, Beijing has aimed to meet its growing and urgent demands for oil and raw materials, curb the United States and European encroachment into its spheres of influence and pave the way for the inflow of Chinese consumer goods into Central Asian markets. Central Asia is of great significance for China as it is a lifeline for transportation and an irreplaceable route heading to Europe and West Asia. Therefore, China proposed the One Belt One Road Initiative or the Belt and Road Initiative (BRI) to revive the ancient Silk Road. It aims, through this new Silk Road, to establish three routes connecting China to Europe)via Central Asia(, the Indian Ocean (via South Asia), the Arabian Gulf and the Mediterranean (via West Asia).

Paul Stronski and Nicole Ng, fellows at the Carnegie Endowment for International Peace, have discussed the policy differences between Beijing, Washington and Moscow toward Central Asia. "Unlike the West, China makes no demands for political reform from Central Asian governments. Unlike Russia, Beijing does not use political pressure to keep the region in its general orientation. The lack of an overt political agenda — other than regional stability, which Beijing believes can be guaranteed through economic development — makes China particularly attractive to local governments."(139)

Unlike its relations with the United States, Iran has good ties with China, on which it depends to counterbalance Washington in the international arena, primarily in Central Asia. China's pragmatic policy toward Central Asia does not pose any serious threat to Iran; it is actually necessary for Iran to have a partner competing with the United States in this region. (140)

The 25-year strategic cooperation agreement was signed in March 2021 and entered into force in 2022. Despite US sanctions being enforced on these two countries, the strategic accord entailed economic, military and security cooperation. [141] Concluding such a long-term strategic accord indicates that China is keen to expand its spheres of influence to reap lucrative economic and investment gains. China is interested in enhancing cooperation with Iran because of its natural resources and strategic location that enables access to the Arabian Gulf, the Arabian Sea and the Indian Ocean. On the other side, Iran has been experiencing many security concerns that have mounted as Washington increased its pressure on its economy due to its activities in the region. Thus, the strategic accord is deemed a lifesaver for Iran that will rescue its deteriorating economy and safeguard its political system from any foreign attacks.

China aspires to establish the new Silk Road passing through Central Asia to Europe. To achieve this goal, China is willing to overcome any obstacles hindering its project. In 2012, China and Tajikistan settled an old border dispute after Dushanbe agreed to cede 1,000 square kilometers of land to Beijing in return for limited preferential economic treatment. They also agreed that China's Dong Ying Heli Investment and Development Co. Ltd would start constructing an oil refinery in the south of Tajikistan.

Many argue that China adopts a pragmatic policy toward Central Asia, especially toward Tajikistan in light of its security considerations. China is determined to establish buffer zones along the border with Afghanistan, Pakistan and Tajikistan, given that its major nagging concern is the growing threat of what it calls "radical Islamism" in the region — which is a source of destabilization in the Xinjiang Uygur Autonomous

Region (XUAR). China has actually set up an anti-terrorism alliance with Pakistan, Afghanistan and Tajikistan to boost coordination with its neighbors to tackle the growing militant threat. Apparently, these countries were urged by China to strengthen their military and security cooperation with it. [142]

Turkey

Iran-Turkey rivalry in Central Asia has mounted to competition over which country proposes the best project in this region. They have fervently worked to boost deep mutual ties — seemingly — with all of the Central Asian republics but within a comprehensive regional framework. Their projects reveal their own ambitions and two main goals: to restructure their neighboring sphere under the auspices of regional cooperation organizations and to recraft the political agenda of the region in a way that helps in developing an intraregional affinity to help in forging their proposed regional blocs.

Since 2002, Turkey has adopted the philosophy of cooperation and partnership toward Central Asia. It presented itself as the big brother, a source of stability and security and a model state for the Central Asian republics, given that five of them are Muslim majority states and have common cultural and historical bonds with Turkey. These factors have created a great opportunity for Turkey and opened a new window for wide-scale relations. Ankara supported Central Asian republics with grants and loans and established many economic, social and educational institutes and attempted to mediate in the Nagorno-Karabakh conflict through the "Caucasus Stability and Cooperation Platform," which was established by Ankara in 2008 following the Russo-Georgian War. Turkey also plays an active role in educational and cultural activities in the region through its network of Turkish schools and universities. As part of Ankara's plans to enhance Turkish identity and culture in the Central Asian republics, a considerable number of Central Asian students attend Turkish universities. This Turkish influence has become a tiresome nuisance for Iranians.

Turkey's moves in this region are marked by its proposal of counter-projects that are completely equal with and parallel to those of Iran. In response to Iran's attempt to ideologize the ECO Turkey hosted the Summit of the Heads of Turkic Speaking States in October 1992; the summit included the Central Asian republics that are culturally and linguistically connected to it. In response to Iran's cooperation project with the Caspian Sea littoral states, Ankara rushed to establish the Black Sea Economic Cooperation Zone (BSECZ), which includes in addition to the Caspian Sea littoral states Alania, Armenia, and Azerbaijan.[143] Turkey's various projects and initiatives are reflective of its dual policy in this region; it attempts to balance between geographical and political considerations, namely as follows:[144]

• Establish a regional cooperation framework — similar to other regional cooperation organizations — with Turkey assuming a pivotal role.

• Highlight the strong presence of common language and culture of Turkic ethnic groups, which is apparent in the membership of Azerbaijan and Albania in BSECZ.

• Foster a conducive political environment to ensure the selection of Turkey's proposal as the best pipeline route to transport Caspian Sea energy compared to Iran's and Russia's proposals.

• Convince the Caspian littoral states that cooperation with Turkey is better than with Iran, given its location as the gateway to the EU and the United States in political and economic terms.

For a greater understanding of Turkey-Iran competition in Central Asia, one needs to take into account their historical and geographical bonds with the region and its geopolitical and economic significance. As for Turkey, it shares a common cultural background with most of the Central Asian republics. The collapse of the Soviet Union beyond a shadow of a doubt opened the gate wide for Turkey to exercise influence in the newly independent republics. Needless to mention that the West was in dire need of Turkey's influence to fill the power vacuum left by the Soviet Union back then. Finally, Turkey was a role model state for the five republics to aspire to in terms of its political model or capitalist orientation, which conflicted with their Soviet legacy of socialism. On the other hand, Iran adopted a sharply contrasting approach to that of Turkey; it proposed its anti-Western theocratic political system. Both Turkey and Iran heavily invested in projects in Central Asia in the struggle for influence in this vital arena. Yet, Turkey's swift penetration into the region would not have been possible without the unconditional support of the United States which aimed to make Ankara a counterweight to Tehran. This was evident in the United States' dependence on Turkey in February 1992 to generate hope among the newly independent former Soviet republics.

Through improving relations with the Central Asian republics, Iran aims to enhance its regional influence and break its international isolation and mitigate the severe sanctions. Turkey, on the other hand, aims to penetrate the region to compensate for its failed attempt to join the EU — part of its strategy to revive its ancient spheres of influence during the Ottoman Empire. Thus, it is logical to conclude that Iran-Turkey competition is not merely over influence and political presence, but also over economic interests and to create a "strategic depth" that serves their objectives and safeguards their interests.

Israel

Tel Aviv aims to penetrate deep into Central Asia through mega projects, providing economic and military aid and intensifying official visits. Having organized the migration of Jewish communities from the Central Asian republics to Israel, Tel Aviv sought to exploit the religious heritage in establishing political, economic and social ties with the region. Official delegations of the Israeli government visited the Central Asian republics where they concluded economic agreements, paving the way for Israeli penetration into this region. The Israeli government established the Chamber of Trade and Industry with Central Asia that supplied economic statistics and served as an Israeli investors' guide to Central Asia. It also developed regulations to protect Israeli investments in Central Asia, in addition to customs exemptions and double taxation. Later on, Israeli companies and Jewish entrepreneurs flocked to Central Asia and managed to open institutes and trade offices that invested in all the fields that they could access. However, their investments mainly focused on energy, mining, agriculture, livestock, industry, banking and finance, human resources, medicine, healthcare and space science research. In Kazakhstan, Israel held a grip over mines and plants that annually produced tons of uranium for use in nuclear weapons. Israel officially purchased a huge complex for uranium processing that could annually produce the amount of uranium needed to manufacture a complete nuclear arsenal. Israel used the Kazakh Baikonur Cosmodrome site to launch more than one satellite into orbit. In return, Kazakhstan gained expertise from Israeli companies in agriculture, particularly in irrigation and the food industry. They also cooperated in oil refining and petrochemicals.[145]

The so-called US-led War on Terror granted Israel a pretext to unleash intensive intelligence and military activities across

Central Asia. In Tashkent, a branch of the Jewish Agency for Israel opened to organize the migration of Uzbek Jews to Israel and a Zionist cultural office was intensively involved in the promotion of Zionist ideology and culture among Jews and other Uzbek citizens in addition to teaching Hebrew. Since the 1990s, Israel's growing penetration into the region rapidly expanded into politics, economy and culture. This penetration helped in developing a solid bedrock for wide-scale security cooperation, especially in the areas of competition with Iran.[146]

The Kingdom of Saudi Arabia

In the early 1990s, Saudi Arabia started to forge relations with the newly independent Central Asian republics but to a limited extent. Bilateral relations were mainly confined to cooperation agreements and memorandums of understanding for political consultations. These were not effectively implemented nor followed up because government apparatuses, back then, did not realize their significance and strategic dimensions. Saudi-Kazakh relations date back to 1994. Riyadh aided the establishment of the Senate of Kazakhstan with $15 billion and concluded nearly 11 trade agreements worth $1.3 billion, in addition to establishing 17 joint institutes.

As for Uzbekistan, relations date back to 1991. A parliamentary joint committee was formed, in addition to concluding a host of agreements on air transportation, sports and youth. Riyadh aided the construction of 959 housing units in Uzbekistan. The two countries sought to increase full-fledged cooperation in petrochemistry, mining, engineering, construction, infrastructure, communication, information technology, education, agriculture and the food industry.[147]

Saudi relations with Turkmenistan date back to 1992. The two countries signed agreements in politics, trade, sports and medicine. They concluded dozens of the most significant agreements and memorandums of understanding in the region, which came into force after the intensification of mutual official visits, nearly every single month there was a mutual official visit.[148]

Having attempted to promote its ideological scheme and Shiite sect through supporting loyalist groups, Iran sought to deeply infiltrate some Central Asian republics. Meanwhile, Saudi Arabia has exerted efforts to counter this Iranian attempt by safeguarding the Sunni republics from the wave of Shiism that Iran has aimed to spread across its surrounding areas. As part of its efforts to curb Iran's role in Sunni areas, Saudi Arabia forged official political and diplomatic ties with Tajikistan on January 11, 1992; a few months following the collapse of the Soviet Union and the declaration of Tajikistan's independence (on September 9, 1991). Former Foreign Saudi Minister Prince Saud Al Faisal paid his first official visit to Dushanbe on February 21, 1992, where he met with former Tajik President Rahmon Nabiyev and a number of high-ranking state officials. Later, Tajik President Rahmon visited Saudi Arabia four times and played a prominent role in boosting amicable relations and establishing fruitful multilateral cooperation. Saudi Arabia developed cooperation in many areas, especially in crime-fighting, education, science, technology, youth affairs, sports and air communication. Significant agreements were concluded for cooperation in the fields of economy, trade, investment, technology, culture, sports and youth affairs.

The Saudi Fund for Development (SFD) contributed to funding infrastructure projects in Tajikistan. Since 2002, the Tajik government has cooperated with SFD and has concluded seven agreements worth 220,122 million Saudi riyals ($58,652,464) that chiefly aim to develop education, health, and road construction.[(149)] As part of their efforts to upgrade and expand their economic relations into wider areas of cooperation, the Saudi-Tajik Business Council was established. The council holds annual meetings and is a subsidiary to the Federation of Saudi Chambers (FSC). The first session was held on June 27, 2022, in the capital of Tajikistan, Dushanbe.

Through economic cooperation, Saudi Arabia sought to counter Iran and halt its Shiite promotion campaign in this Islamic country that is at the heart of Asia. It is worth noting that there are 3,348 mosques, 330 prominent mosques (jam-e-masjid; Friday prayer mosques), 34 central mosques, three Islamic schools and one Islamic center in Tajikistan.[(150)]

Saudi Arabia intended to invest in Turkmenistan's gas transportation sector and include this significant Central Asian republic in OPEC as an observer state. Accordingly, Saudi Arabia's step will add a new dimension to the competition over the transportation of Turkmenistan gas. This dimension will see Turkmenistan more intertwined with the Middle Eastern countries through its association with OPEC. If Saudi Arabia is eager to transport Turkmenistan gas it will choose to back the Turkmenistan–Afghanistan–Pakistan–India (TAPI) pipeline project. This is due to the fact that Pakistan and India are in dire need of gas and have not reached a bilateral or trilateral agreement with Afghanistan to implement the pipeline, given their thorny political issues. Thus, having Saudi Arabia become a competitor with global powers for Turkmenistan's gas, Iran's influence and ability to negotiate with Pakistan regarding the latter's positions on the Middle East will decline while Saudi Arabia's relations with India, Pakistan and Afghanistan will be boosted further.

CONCLUSION

Iran's policy toward Central Asia and the South Caucasus is based on a host of political, economic and security considerations. Through this policy, Iran managed to establish good ties with the South Caucasus nations, namely Armenia whose expanding relations and cooperation with Iran developed into a partnership. On the contrary, Iran's relations with Azerbaijan have been often marked by tensions and instability due to their longstanding disagreements, most prominently the disagreement over the division of the Caspian Sea's resources, the Azeri minority in Iran and Tehran's alignment with Yerevan in the Nagorno-Karabakh conflict. Iran, however, sought to open up toward Azerbaijan and improve its relations with an aim to invest in its oil resources in the Caspian Sea.

In Central Asia, Iran sought to be the most influential actor, exploiting its geographical affinity, common history and intra-regional economic need. But, following the collapse of the Soviet Union, Iran's influence was greatly limited at all levels (political, ideological and cultural) in Central Asia's newly independent republics; most probably because of their secular outlook and rampant intra-nationalism. Needless to say, they aspired to be liberated from religious and cultural strife and foreign interventions in their internal affairs. Economic challenges have also obstructed Iran's influence there. Tehran has been experiencing economic woes because of international sanctions. One also needs to consider the fierce competition between regional and global powers for influence in Central

Asia and their attempts to achieve dominance along with establishing the largest economic and investment projects in the region.

The governments of Central Asia and the South Caucasus have experienced shifts in their foreign policies and drastic transformations in their perceptions over the last decade. They do not view themselves anymore as isolated and landlocked with complete reliance on Russia and Iran for foreign affairs. The mounting presence of the United States, China, Turkey and the Gulf states made these republics realize their worth and offered them much wider options to pick and choose their partners as well as to take up the most attractive opportunities — apparently, Iran missed the boat here.

Iran's presence has faced snowballing obstacles in this region due to the reimposition of sanctions against the backdrop of its nuclear program. In the first quarter of 2019, Iran's trade in general witnessed a sharp decline, which was primarily attributed to the decline in oil exports and non-oil imports after the United States imposed its second round of sanctions in November 2018. Iran's exports to some countries hit zero while imports witnessed an unprecedented fall, nearly 60 percent. Since the US withdrawal from the nuclear deal in May 2018, Iranian exports of crude oil declined to 50 percent and reached 500 barrels per day by the end of June 2019.

The world powers and Iran have not reached an agreement regarding the latter's nuclear and ballistic missile programs and neither on its support for sectarian militias. Thus, as long as Iran's thorny issues are not resolved, it will continue to experience a dangerous recession, and further international isolation that will not only cast a shadow on its presence in Central Asia and the Caucasus but also on its foreign relations across the Middle East and beyond. This political and economic stagnation will probably result in the decline of Iran's position in the comprehensive regional balance of power equation; its impact on crises and wars in the Middle East, especially the endurance of its proxy wars will also start to fade away.

On a final note, the ideological principles of the Iranian republic, its theocratic ruling system; the policies of the Wilayat al-Faqih ruling system toward neighbors have all impacted the nature of Iran's relations toward Central Asia. Iran has been unable to forge good ties with the Central Asian republics because of: the fundamentals of the 1979 revolution that have shaped Iran's foreign policy; whether in terms of exporting the revolution under the pretext of the need to help the "oppressed" or its interventions in the domestic affairs of other countries through enclaves of pro-Iran parties that operate outside the official framework of foreign relations.

ENDNOTES

(1) Ibrahim Arafat, "Central Asia: The International Competition in a Landlocked Region," *Al Siyassa Al Dawliya*, no. 167 (January 2007): 125. [Arabic].

(2) Raya Khouri, "Central Asia in Great Power Conflict," *Geopolitika*, May 5, 2016, accessed June 13, 2019, https://bit.ly/٣١u٢tf٤. [Arabic].

(3) Karam Sahlab, "What Are the Caucasus Countries?" *Mawdoo3*, accessed May 1, 2019, http://cutt.us/hIv%D9%A4e. [Arabic].

(4) "Asian Studies," *Loyola University Chicago*, accessed February 14, 2023, https://bit.ly/3JfG6xP.

(5) Hanan Abu Sekeen, "Between Conflict and Cooperation: International Competition in Central Asia," *Arab Center for Research and Studies*, June 10, 2014, accessed May 1, 2019, http://cutt.us/zNGxS. [Arabic].

(6) Mehradad Mohsenin, "Iran's Relation With Central Asia and the Caucasus," *The Iranian Journal of Internationals Affairs* 7, no.4 (1996).

(7) Fred Halliday, "Condemned to React Unable Influence: Iran and Transcausus, in John F.R. Wright and Suzzane Goldenberg eds., *Transcaucasian Boundaries* (UCL Press Limited, London, 1996), 73.

(8) Mohsenin, "Iran's Relation With Central Asia and the Caucasus," 35-37.

(9) Edmund Herzig, *Iran and the Former Soviet South* (London: The Royal Institute of International Affairs, 1995), 2-3.

(10) Salah al-Saifi, "The Caspian Sea Oil and Great Power Conflict (Oil, Politics, and Blood)," *Islamtoday*, June 6, 2007, accessed May 1, 2009, http://cutt.us/vlJuK. [Arabic].

(11) R.K. Ramazani, "Iran's Foreign Policy: Both North and South," *Middle East Journal* 46, no. 3 (Summer 1992): 393, http://www.jstor.org/stable/4328462.

(12) Ibid., 4001-410.

(13) V. Mesamed, "Iran: Ten Years in Post-Soviet Central Asia," *Central Asia and the Caucasus* April 17, 2019, accessed May 1, 2019, https://bit.ly/2RbbxhA.

(14) Yasser Qassir ed., "Geopolitical Transformations and Security in Iran (Seminar)," *Middle Eastern Affairs Journal* 84, (June 1999): 40. [Arabic].

(15) Tahir Shir Mohammadi,"The Islamic Revolution of Iran and Former Soviet Muslim Republics," *DW*, November 18, 2017, accessed May 1, 2019, https://cutt.us/yxSUn.

(16) Abu Sekeen, "Between Conflict and Cooperation."

(17) Helmut Schmidt, "Book Review of The Grand Chessboard: American Primacy and Its Geostrategic Imperatives," *Foreign Policy*, (Spring 1998), https://ciaotest.cc.columbia.edu/olj/fp/schmidt.html.

(18) Mohammed Shakir, "Iran-Tajikistan Relations Internal and External Challenges," *Journal for Iranian Studies* 2, no. 5 (December 2017), https://bit.ly/3Zg7eSX.

(19) Mohammed bin Abdulrahman al-Obaidi, "Iran and Republics of Caucasus Region (Study on the Political and Economic Relations 1991-2008)," *Regional Studies Journal* 6, no. 14 (2009): 184-195, accessed June 10, 2019, https://bit.ly/2Zjfhim.[Arabic]. See Ammar Jafal, *Turkey-Iran Competition in Central Asia* (Abu Dhabi: Emirates Center for Strategic Studies and Research, 2005), 62-63. [Arabic].

(20) Sebastien Peyrouse, "Iran's Growing Role in Central Asia? Geopolitical, Economic and Political Profit and Loss Account," *Al Jazeera Center for Studies*, April 14, 2014, accessed April 23, 2019, http://bit.ly/3y22yE9.

(21) Qassir, "Geopolitical Transformations and Security in Iran."

(22) Roman Muzalevsky, "The 'Persian Alliance' and Geopolitical Reconfiguration in Central Asia," *The James Town Foundation*, April 17, 2019, accessed August 23, 2022, http://cutt.us/raky6.

(23) "History," *ECO*, accessed August 23, 2022, https://bit.ly/3TclEkk.

(24) "Frequently Asked Questions," *SCO*, accessed August 23, 2022, http://eng.sectsco.org/docs/about/faq.html.

(25) Ibid.

(26) Houman A. Sadri and Nader Entessar, "Iranian-Azeri Dynamic Relations: Conflict & Cooperation in Southern Caucasus1," *Rivista di Studi Politici Internazionali* 76, no. 1 (301) (2009): 61, http://www.jstor.org/stable/42740780.

(27) Ali Akbar Velayati, The Islamic Republic of Iran, Central Asia and the Caucasus, Speech delivered at the Crans -Montana Forum, Switzerland, 20-23 June 1996.

(28) Ramazani, "Iran's Foreign Policy: Both North and South," 408.

(29) N.J. Watson, "Not Yet a Caspian Sea Change," *Petroleum Economist* 73, no. 10, (October 2006): 32.

(30) Jerzy Rohozinski, "Religious Rebirth in Azerbaijan," *World Press Review* 48, no. 4 (April 2001): 38-39; and Kevin Whitelaw, "Refugee: 1 in 10 Azerbaijanis," *US News & World Report* 123, (November 13, 1997): 64-65.

(31) "Iran Announces Its Readiness to Mediate Between Armenia and Azerbaijan," *Sputnik*, September 10, 2022., accessed August 11, 2022, https://bit.ly/3fNBflm.

(32) *Iran Times*, (February 18, 1994), 16; and *Iran Times* (March), 16.

(33) *Kayhan Havai*, May 25, 1994, 32, and *Iran Times*, 8 July 1994, 14.

(34) Tamine Adeebfar, "Azerbaijan's Geopolitical Challenge," *Middle East Economic Survey* 49, December 4, 2006.

(35) Marzieh Kouhi Esfahani, *Iran's Foreign Policy in the South Caucasus: Relations with Azerbaijan and Armenia* (London & New York: Routledge, 2019), 9.

(36) Habibuallah Abu al-Hassan Shirazi, "The Development of Iran's Relations With Central Asia: Strategies," *Geography and Development*, (Spring & Summer 1384). [Persian].

(37) Peimani, *Iran and the United States*, 20.

(38) Hooman Peimani, *Regional Security and the Future of Central Asia: the Competition of Iran, Turkey, and Russia,* Westport, Conn: Praeger, 1998, 80.

(39) Nazrin Mehdiyeva, "Azerbaijan & Its Foreign Policy Dilemma," *Asian Affairs* 34, no. 3 (November 2003): 271-285.

(40) *Iran Times,* March 8, 1996, 1.

(41) Huda al-Hosseini, "Iran Is Active to Transform Azerbaijan to Another Iraq," *Asharq AlAwsat*, June 25, 2018, accessed May 6, 2019, https://bit.ly/2LoXvZ5. [Arabic].

(42) "Development of Iran-Azerbaijan Relations (1991-2016)," *Al-Mawqif,* accessed June 13, 2019, https://bit.ly/2XdaPnW. [Arabic].

(43) "The Challenge to Salafisim in Central Asia and the Caucasus," *Al-Bayan,* accessed April 2, 2019, http://cutt.us/kEsHn. [Arabic].

(44) M. Luomi, "Sectarian Identities or Geopolitics? The Regional Shia-Sunni Divide in the Middle East, " *FIIIA Working Paper*, no. 56 (2008), accessed April 7, 2019, http://cutt.us/rkoNS.

(45) Mohammed al-Sayyed Selim, *Mukhtarat Iraniya (Iranian Selections)* 9, (April 2001), quoted from *Al-Bainah*, https://bit.ly/2IzzBWc. [Arabic].

(46) Joseph S. Nye, Jr., "Public Diplomacy in a Changing World," *The Annals of the American Academy of Political and Social Science 616*, (March 2008): 97, https://www.jstor.org/stable/25097996.

(47) Ayman Saleh, "Tajikistan Warns Iran of Continuing on Shiism Amongst Tajik Youth," *EREM News,* October 26, 2017, accessed July 10, 2019, https://bit.ly/2ZmxLih. [Arabic].

(48) "Iran and Tajikistan Sign 9 Protocols for Mutual Cooperation," *IRNA*, April 2002, accessed January 30, 2022, https://bit.ly/3T0gpos.

(49) Post on *Network of Defending Sunnis*, April 4, 2009 accessed July 10, 2019, https://bit.ly/2XAyCeE. [Arabic].

(50) Mohammed Alsulami, "Iran's Terrorism Between Tajikistan and Afghanistan," *Al Watan*, August 17, 2017, accessed April 2, 2019, http://cutt.us/Cvh1c. [Arabic].

(51) Ibid.

(52) M. Mesbahi, "Tajikistan, Iran and the International Politics of the 'Islamic Factor', " *Central Asian Survey* 16, no. 2 (1997): 141.

(53) Ilia Jazare'ri, "Tajakestan: Shutting Down Iranian Offices and Banning Publications," *Al Arabiya*, a accessed May 5, 2019, http://cutt.us/TAsgu. [Arabic].

(54) Kazaz Mahdi Hafteh, "Central Asia, World and Regional Powers With an Emphasis On Iran," *Journal of Economic and Social Research* 18, Special Issue 2 (2019): 124-129.

(55) Ali al-Quhis, "Review on Turkey-Iran Competition in Central Asia and the Caucasus," *Al Riyadh*, May 19, 2005, accessed June 10, 2019, https://bit.ly/2KbTgys. [Arabic].

(56) "Greater Azerbaijan," *Scribble Maps*, accessed February 14, 2023, http://bit.ly/3Yx4Aa5.

(57) Houman Sadri and Nader Entessar. "Iranian-Azeri Dynamic Relations: Conflict & Cooperation in Southern Caucasus." *Rivista Di Studi Politici Internazionali* 76, no. 1 (301) (2009): 59–79. http://www.jstor.org/stable/42740780.

(58) *Kayhan Havai*, October 12, 1998, 17.

(59) *Agence France Presse* (AFP), January 18, 2008.

(60) Mehrdad Mohsenin," Iran's Regional Role in the Future of Central Asia: The Case of Iran- Turkmenistan Relations," *Central Asia and the Caucasus Journal (IPIS)* 5, no. 2 (Winter 1996), https://bit.ly/35aQEsl. [Persian].

(61) Jafal, *Turkey-Iran Competition in Central Asia*, 62-63.

(62) Shirazi, "The Development of Iran's Relations With Central Asia."

(63) Ibid.

(64) Ibid.

(65) Jafal, 64.

(66) "Tajikistan and Iran : Is Dushanbe Distancing Itself From Cultural Cousin?," *Eurasianet*, March 7, 2011, accessed April 7, 2019, http://cutt.us/7Ovnh.

(67) Sebastien Peyrouse, "Shiism in Central Asia : The Religious, Political, and Geopolitical Factors," *The Central Asia and Caucasus Analyst*, May 20, 2009, accessed April 7, 2019, http://cutt.us/6RuTX.

(68) Emad Qumayhah, "Iran Will Not Torture Armenia Twice," *New Lebanon*, April 13, 2016, accessed 6 June, 2019, https://bit.ly/2JiS9fm. [Arabic].

(69) Ibid.

(70) Khair el-Din Haseeb, *Arab-Iranian Relations)* Beirut: Centre for Arab Unity Studies, 1998(, 145-146. [Arabic].

(71) Jafal, 106 and 55.

(72) Mohsenin, "Iran's Relation with Central Asia and the Caucasus," 36-37.

(73) Nasser al-Hazzani, "Does Iran Seek to Expand Its Influence in Central Asia?," *Makkah Newspaper*, December 21, 2017, accessed May 1, 2019, http://cutt.us/8xolH. [Arabic].

(74) Mohsenin, 837.

(75) Hooman Peimani, *Iran and the United States : The Rise of the West Asian Regional Grouping* (USA: Praeger Publishers, 1999), 17.

(76) Herzig, *Iran and the Former Soviet South*, 50.

(77) Halliday, "Condemned to React, Unable to influence," 74.

(78) "Azerbaijan Angers Iran by Recalling Its Occupied South," *Al Arabiya*, April 2, 2013, accessed August 10, 2020, https://bit.ly/3pHwkx6. [Arabic].

(79) "Kayhan Called for a Referendum on the Accession of the Republic of Azerbaijan to Iran," *Radio Farda*, March 21, 2013, accessed August 10, 2020, https://bit.ly/3IkUYtU. [Persian].

(80) "Memoirs and Words of Atash Afroz Hossein Shariatmadari and Mansour Hakitpour About Azerbaijan," *RFI*, March 4, 2013, accessed August 10, 2020, https://bit.ly/3Meqvik. [Persian].

(81) Khavaud Ferydown, "Les Nouvelles Orientation de la Politique Économique Regional de l'Iran," *Cahier d'Études sur la Méditerranée Oriental et le Monde-Turco-Iranian*, no. 15, (January –February 1993): 33. [French].

(82) Abdullah al-Madani, "The Caspian Sea Agreement: Who Is the Loser?" *Alittihad*, September 1, 2018, accessed May 2, 2019, http://eti.ae/BLnC. [Arabic].

(83) "The Sixth Caspian Summit Was Held In Ashgabat," *Ministry of Foreign Affairs of Turkmenistan*, June 30, 2022, accessed February 7, 2023,https://www.mfa.gov.tm/en/news/3233.

(84) "Oil and Natural Gas Production Is Growing in Caspian Sea Region," *US Energy Information Administration*, accessed April 12, 2020. https://bit.ly/2V71M6q.

(85) Diyari Saleh Majeed, *International Competition for Oil Transportation Pipeline Tracks from the Caspian Sea* (Abu Dhabi: Emirates Center for Strategic Studies and Research, 2012), 225. [Arabic].

(86) Ibid., 226.

(87) Quoted from Luke Coffey, "A Secure and Stable Caspian Sea Is in America's Interest," Backgrounder, no. 3070 (December 4, 2025), https://herit.ag/3kQweBd.

(88) Jana Barysaŭna, "The Caspian Sea and Disagreements on Its Resources," *Al Bayan*, July 23, 2011, accessed April 15, 2019, http://cutt.us/cJQgk. [Arabic].

(89) Barclay Ballard, "More Than Sea-mantics: The Legal Status of the Caspian Sea," *BD Destinations*, March 22, 2019, accessed January 25, 2023, http://bit.ly/3yi5mgL.

(90) Madani, "The Caspian Sea Agreement."

(91) Ibid.

(92) David O'Byrne, "With Draft Convention, Resolution of Caspian Sea Status Appears Closer Than Ever," *Eurasianet*, January 27, 2018, accessed January 25, 2023, https://bit.ly/3F5vLCg.

(93) Barysaŭna, "The Caspian Sea and Disagreements on Its Resources."

(94) Mute'e Ta'eballah, "China, Iran, Turkey: The New Players in Central Asia," *Al Jazeera Research Center*, August 12, 2007, accessed April 28, 2019, http://cutt.us/kbyOl.

(95) Ibid.

(96) Mohsenin, "Iran's Relation with Central Asia and the Caucasus," 132.

(97) Peimani, *Regional Security and the Future of Central Asia*, 95.

(98) Nader Entessar, *Iran: Geopolitical Challenges and the Caspian Region* (London: Praeger publishers, 1999), 170.

(99) Peimani, *Regional Security and the Future of Central Asia*, 61-62.

(100) Ibid., 62.

(101) "Iran Ready to Host Russian Oil Tankers," *TiNN*, January 2, 2017, accessed February 14, 2022, https://bit.ly/3J5ZrjY.

(102) "Country Analysis Executive Summary: Iran," *EIA*, accessed April 30, 2019, http://cutt.us/aE9ys.

(103) Ibid.

(104) "Iranian News," *The Iranian*, accessed April 30, 2019, https://bit.ly/39K3AGp.

(105) Entessar, *Iran*, 172.

(106) Peimani, *Regional Security and the Future of Central Asia*. 107-108.

(107) Herzig, *Iran and the Former Soviet South*, 34.

(108) Ibid., 39.

(109) Pier Paolo Raimondi, "Central Asia Oil and Gas Industry-The External Powers' Energy Interests in Kazakhstan, Turkmenistan and Uzbekistan," *Fondazione Eni Enrico Mattei FEEM*, (2019), accessed February 11, 2023, http://www.jstor.com/stable/resrep21861.14.

(110) Bassel Alhaj Jassim, "Exploring the Relations of Central Asia With America and Iran," *Independent Persian*, February 11, 2020, accessed January 25, 2023, https://bit.ly/2RbJkqE. [Persian].

(111) Seyed Kazem Sajjadpour, *Iran, The Caucasus and Central Asia : The New Geopolitics of Central Asia and Its Border Land* (USA: Indiana University Press, 1994), 199.

(112) Herzig, 36.

(113) Sébastien Peyrouse, "Central Asia's Growing Partnership With China," *EUCAM Working Paper*, no. 4 (October 2009), accessed February 14, 2023 https://www.files.ethz.ch/isn/111372/WP4-EN.pdf.

(114) Raimondi, "Central Asia Oil and Gas Industry."

(115) Hooshang E. Chehabi, "Ardabil Becomes a Province: Center-Periphery Relations in Iran," *International Journal of the Middle East Studies* 29, (May 1997): 235-23.

(116) "Water Tender Issues: East Azerbaijan Regional Water Corporation Contract," *Middle East Economic Digest* 51, no.8, (February 23, 2007): 23

(117) As reported *by International Railway Journal*, April 1, 2006.

(118) Ibid.

(119) Kianoush Jamakoohi, Elham Alizadeh, and Hossien Moghimi Esfandabadi, "Analyzing the Capacity of Iran Non-Oil Exports to the Region," *Scientific Research Publishing* 11, no. 2 (2019): 57-65.

(120) Ibid.

(121) Mustafa Barakat, "New Tri-attack: Does North South Corridor Threaten Suez Canal?" *Vetogate*, November 1, 2018, accessed April 30, 2019, http://cutt.us/LXTjh. [Arabic].

(122) Mohammad Fayez Farhat, "North-South Corridor: The Limits of Iranian Power," *Journal for Iranian Studies (JIS)* 2, no. 7 (June 2018), accessed April 2, 2019, https://bit.ly/3EWF8Eg.

(123) Ibid.

(124) "Iran and Turkmenistan Sign Protocol for Rail Cooperation," *Fars News Agency,* April 13, 2018, accessed April 2, 2019, https://bit.ly/3ZHLuz1. [Arabic].

(125) Farhat, "North-South Corridor."

(126) Ibid.

(127) "India, Iran, Russia push alternative to Suez Canal," *Payvand*, October 31, 2018, accessed November 1, 2022, http://bit.ly/3kX5oaM.

(128) Barakati Ghobta, "Port War and the Sea Route Between India and Pakistan," *Asharq Al Awasat*, March 1, 2017, accessed June 9, 2019, https://bit.ly/2ZajpkE. [Arabic].

(129) "Backgrounder: Iran's Chabahar Port," *Geopolitical Monitor*, February 5, 2019, accessed February 25, 2023, http://bit.ly/3KutqEo.

(130) Farhat.

(131) "Discuss Launching a Corridor for International Transport Between North and South as an Alternative to the Suez Canal," *El Mawke3 News*, November 1, 2018, accessed June 16, 2019, https://bit.ly/2WGFPZb. [Arabic].

(132) Mortaza al- Shazili, "Hidden Reasons Behind Excluding Chabahar Port From US Sanctions," *Noon Post*, accessed June 16, 2019, http://cutt.us/cLurA. [Arabic].

(133) "US Waives Sanctions for Iran's Chabahar Port Project," *Maritime Executive*, November 8, 2018, accessed November 25, 2022, http://bit.ly/3ZcpeNG.

(134) Abu Sekeen, "Between Conflict and Cooperation."

(135) Ibid.

(136) "Russia presents Tajikistan with a Shipment of Heavy Weapons," *UAWIRE*, December 20, 2017, accessed January 25, 2022, http://bit.ly/3KIzRUe. "Russia

delivers military equipment to Tajikistan," *Anadolu Agency*, December 19, 2017, accessed January 25, 2022, https://bit.ly/3EE4jLx.

(137) Mahmoud Dehghan Terzjani, "Priorities and Sources of Threats to Iran's National Interests in Central Asia and the Caucasus," *Political and Economic Information* 1378, no. 145 and 146 (October and November 1999), https://bit.ly/3L4ae0u. [Persian].

(138) Abu Sekeen.

(139) Paul Stronski and Nicole Ng, "Cooperation and Competition, Russia and China in Central Asia, the Russian Far East, and the Arctic," *Carnegie Endowment for International Peace*, February 28, 2018, accessed February 14, 2023, https://bit.ly/3L7tWsm.

(140) Harold Scott W. and Alireza Nader, "China and Iran: Economic, Political, and Military Relations" (Santa Monica, CA: RAND Corporation, 2012), https://www.rand.org/pubs/occasional_papers/OP351.html.

(141) Maziar Motamedi, "Iran Says 25-year China Agreement Enters Implementation Stage," *Al Jazeera*, January 15, 2022, accessed May 10, 2023, https://bit.ly/3pNWcrg.

(142) Abu Sekeen.

(143) Gresh Alain, "La Zone de Coopération conomique des Pays Riverains de la Mer Noire," (The Economic Cooperation Zone of the Countries Bordering the Black Sea), *Cahiers d'Études sur la Méditerranée Orientale*, (November 1993): 39. [French].

(144) Jafal, 65.

(145) Abu Sekeen.

(146) Ibid.

(147) "Saudi Arabia and Kazakhstan to Enhance Trade and Investment Relations," *Al Hayat*, accessed June 23, 2019, https://bit.ly/2WYSIhi.

(148) Jodah Abu al-Nour, "Saudi Ambassador to Turkmenistan Appreciates the Bilateral Relations Between the Two Countries and Praises His Country's Ties with Cairo," *Al Ahram*, June 21, 2017, accessed June 23, 2019, https://bit.ly/2XwmxKD. [Arabic].

(149) "Relations Between the Republic of Tajikistan and the Kingdom of Saudi Arabia, " *Embassy of the Republic Tajikistan in the Kingdom of Saudi Arabia*, accessed June 23, 2019, https://bit.ly/2WYSIhi.

(150) "President of Tajikistan: King Abdullah Gave a Strong Impetus to Relations Between the Two Countries," *Al Riyadh*, July 6, 2011, accessed June 23, 2019, https://bit.ly/2Y52dx7. [Arabic].

ABOUT THE AUTHOR

Ahmed al-Garni is an expert in strategic studies and holds a doctorate in International Relations from Sorbonne University. He is the vice president of Rasanah IIIS and an academic visitor to Oxford University. Garni has published several research articles and books, including *Towards a New Strategic Thinking Leading in a Chaotic and Dynamic World*.